GIVE THANKS WITH A
GRATEFUL HEART

INTEGRITY
PUBLISHERS'

GIVE THANKS WITH A GRATEFUL HEART

Devotions copyright © 2002, Integrity Publishers. Devotions written by Greg Asimakoupoulos.

Published by Integrity Publishers, a division of Integrity Media, Inc., 5250 Virginia Way, Suite 110, Brentwood, TN 37027.

Unless otherwise indicated, Scripture quotations used in this book are from the Holy Bible, New International Version (NIV). Copyright © 1973, 1978, 1984 by International Bible Society. Used by permission of Zondervan Publishing House. All rights reserved.

Other Scripture quotations are from the following sources:

Scripture quotations marked (NLT) are taken from the Holy Bible, New Living Translation, copyright © 1996. Used by permission of Tyndale House Publishers, Inc., Wheaton, Illinois 60189. All rights reserved.

Scripture quotations marked (NASB) are taken from the New American Standard Bible, copyright © 1960, 1977 by the Lockman Foundation. All rights reserved.

Scripture quotations marked (KJV) are taken from the Holy Bible, King James Version.

Scripture quotations marked (NKJV) are taken from the Holy Bible, New King James Version, copyright © 1982 by Thomas Nelson, Inc. All rights reserved.

Produced with the assistance of The Livingstone Corporation. Project staff includes David Veerman, Neil Wilson, Linda Taylor, Ashley Taylor.

Interior design/Cover design by The Office of Bill Chiaravalle | www.officeofbc.com.

ISBN 1-59145-022-5

Printed in the United States of America

05 06 RRD 5 4 3

TABLE OF CONTENTS

INTRODUCTION

Our gracious and holy God desires gratitude from his people. And who more deserves our gratitude and praise than the One who blesses us abundantly with life and joy and hope?

An exciting and appropriate way to express our heartfelt love and thanks to God is through glorious songs of worship. As the Bible tells us, "Sing psalms, hymns and spiritual songs with gratitude in your heart to God" (Colossians 3:16b, NIV).

Give Thanks with a Grateful Heart is a majestic and moving daily devotional based on a collection of the most powerful praise and worship songs of all time. The beautiful lyrics will lift your spirits, express for you the feelings you may have difficulty expressing, and allow you to experience God's saving grace and amazing love.

Why not spend a few minutes alone with God each day by focusing on one of these magnificent songs of praise and thanksgiving to him? Sing the song, read God's Word, pray reverently to him. Give thanks to him with a grateful heart. Then rejoice as God responds in love to your gratitude with even more rich blessings. The time you spend in devotion to him will undoubtedly be the most exceptional moments of your day.

May God continue to bless you as you express your thanks and love to him each day of your life.

D A Y   1

G I V E   T H A N K S   W I T H   A
G R A T E F U L   H E A R T

Give thanks with a grateful heart,
Give thanks to the Holy One,
Give thanks because He's given
Jesus Christ, His Son.

And now, let the weak say, "I am strong,"
Let the poor say, "I am rich,
Because of what
The Lord has done for us."
Give thanks.

—HENRY SMITH

ive thanks. To whom? The Holy One, God Himself. Why?

Because He has given Jesus Christ, His Son. Given Him for what? To die on a cross and save us from our sins. Give thanks. How? With a grateful heart.

If we really think about it, we are overwhelmed. God sent His one and only Son to die a cruel death on a cross. That's how much He loves us—rebellious, evil, contentious, sinful people. We don't deserve such love. We don't deserve to have someone die for us—and yet Someone did. God looked down upon His glorious creation, now stained by sin, and He knew He would act to bring us back to Himself. He could not simply overlook sin, change His mind, or decide that maybe sin isn't so bad after all. Sin had to be punished, but He took the punishment upon Himself through His Son. When Jesus shed His blood on the cross, He was paying the punishment for our sins. Now, when we accept His sacrifice, we are made right with God.

Give thanks, and do so with a grateful heart! We would have no hope for eternity if not for the Holy One who has given Jesus Christ, His Son, for us.

For God so loved the world that he gave his one and only Son, that whoever believes in him shall not perish but have eternal life.

JOHN 3:16

PRAYER

Thank the Lord for giving Jesus Christ, His Son, to take the punishment your sins deserved. Thank Him with a grateful heart for all He has done for you.

A L M I G H T Y

Almighty, Most Holy God—
Faithful through the ages.
Almighty, Most Holy Lord—
Glorious, Almighty God.

The beasts of the field,
The birds of the air
Are silent to call out Your name.
The earth has no voice,
And I have no choice
But to magnify God unashamed.
Let the rocks be kept silent
For one more day.
Let the whole world sing out;
Let the people say . . .

—WAYNE WATSON

mother asked her preschool daughter, "What are you drawing a picture of?"

The little girl unabashedly replied, "I'm drawing God!"

"But, sweetheart, no one knows what God looks like."

Continuing to pull her pencil across her tablet, the young artist
sighed, "They will when I'm done!"

Try to explain God and you'll quickly discover that you're in
over your head. Nobody can explain who God is, what He looks like,
why He works as He does. Yet when Jesus draped himself in human
skin and entered our world, He gave us a glimpse of God. The apostle
John put it this way: "The Word became flesh and made his dwelling
among us" (John 1:14).

But that was two millennia ago. What about when the "Word"
doesn't become flesh but simply remains a book on the table? Well,
that's when we need to open that book and discover for ourselves
more about God. We may not be able to see God, but when we look
into His Word, we learn what He is like. We discover, among other
things, that He is almighty, glorious, most holy, faithful. What adjectives
can you add to the list?

*Now to the King eternal, immortal, invisible, the only God, be honor and glory for ever
and ever. Amen.*

1 TIMOTHY 1:17

PRAYER

Spend some quiet moments in the Father's presence. As you ponder His creation, consider how the Lord
has earned the titles "almighty," "holy," and "faithful."

5

DAY 3

VICTORY CHANT

Hail, Jesus! You're my King;
Your life frees me to sing;
I will praise You all my days;
You're perfect in all Your ways.

Hail, hail, Lion of Judah!
How powerful You are.
Hail, hail, Lion of Judah!
How wonderful You are.

—JOSEPH VOGEL

othing is quite like a college football stadium when the home team comes from behind to win the game. The rhythm of pounding drums echoes through the stands. The stomps and cheers of approving fans are thunderously loud. An amazing victory demands an appropriate response.

Christians have even more reason to celebrate. What Jesus accomplished on the cross was far more important than any game. Although He was sidelined for three days, He returned from the grave to erase any doubt as to what He had done. Once and for all, Jesus won our eternal salvation and defeated death. But the King of kings not only conquered death, He invaded our self-centered hearts, freeing us from ourselves.

So we owe Him our praise. We hail Him—Lion of the tribe of Judah—who will one day open the scrolls and usher the end of history as we know it. And we will be with Him forever because of what He has done for us. It's our privilege to celebrate His victory with songs of praise, expressions of joy, and prayers of gratitude. His love truly does free us to sing. So how about it? Have you sung yet today?

Then one of the elders said to me, "Do not weep! See, the Lion of the tribe of Judah, the Root of David, has triumphed. He is able to open the scroll and its seven seals."

REVELATION 5:5

PRAYER

Repeat the first phrase of "Victory Chant" over and over aloud. Thank Him for freeing you to sing praises to Him.

J E S U S   I S   A L I V E !

Hallelujah!

Jesus is alive.

Death has lost its vict'ry

And the grave has been denied.

Jesus lives forever!

He's alive!

He's alive!

—RON KENOLY

eople of all ages gathered in a small Baptist church in rural Bangladesh to view a screening of the "Jesus" film. The small building was so crowded that little children had to sit on the floor while rows of adults stood in the back. During the crucifixion scene, weeping and gasps of disbelief could be heard as the dark-skinned audience looked on in horror. As the Bengalis watched, they vicariously sensed the drama of the moment. It was as if they actually could feel the agony of Jesus' pain and the disappointment of the disciples. In that emotional moment, one young boy near the makeshift screen jumped to his feet and cried out, "Don't be afraid. He gets up again! I saw the movie before."

Whether we say, "He gets up again," "Christ is risen," or "He's alive!" the reality of the resurrection should not be reserved for only one Sunday a year. The message of Easter is the foundation of our faith every single day of our lives. Because Jesus defeated death, He is not bound by space, time, or distance. He's alive! Jesus lives forever! Write in block letters across your calendar, "EVERY DAY IS EASTER!"

Because Jesus lives forever, he has a permanent priesthood. Therefore he is able to save completely those who come to God through him, because he always lives to intercede for them.

HEBREWS 7:24, 25

PRAYER

Spend some quiet moments rehearsing the "crosses" you are currently carrying in your life. Then thank Jesus that because His cross did not defeat Him, so He is alive today to help you carry yours.

M O U R N I N G   I N T O   D A N C I N G

He's turned my mourning into dancing again;

He lifted my sorrows.

I can't stay silent;

I must sing for His joy has come.

—TOMMY WALKER

ourning. Unless you see it spelled, the mere mention of the word suggests the delight of a breathtaking sunrise or the fresh start each daybreak promises. In reality, however, "mourning" means just the opposite. Those who mourn are sorrowing. Their soul is lost in a long (and seemingly endless) night.

Mourning is part of life in an imperfect world. The Bible tells us that "the wages of sin is death" (Romans 6:23). When sin came into the world, death tagged along. When death takes loved ones, we mourn. That is a natural process—we should. In fact, it is healthy to grieve for a time. There is indeed "a time to weep and a time to laugh, a time to mourn and a time to dance" (Ecclesiastes 3:4).

Of course, we will miss the person and feel the sorrow, but in the midst of mourning, God promises daily mercy and grace. The time for laughter and dancing will return, for God will lift our sorrows. He approaches us and asks us to dance. Though circumstances may be difficult, He alone can waltz us away from the brink of despair and envelop us with His everlasting arms.

Then maidens will dance and be glad, young men and old as well. I will turn their mourning into gladness; I will give them comfort and joy instead of sorrow.

JEREMIAH 31:13

PRAYER

If you are in mourning because of some loss in your life, pour out your heart to the Lord. Admit your feelings candidly. Ask Him to sweep you off your feet with a sense of His presence.

GREAT IS THE LORD

Great is the Lord, He is holy and just.

By His power we trust in His love.

Great is the Lord, He is faithful and true.

By His mercy He proves He is love.

Great are You, Lord, and worthy of glory!

Great are You, Lord, and worthy of praise!

Great are You, Lord!

I lift up my voice;

I lift up my voice.

Great are You, Lord!

—MICHAEL W. SMITH AND DEBORAH SMITH

emember playing with a magnifying glass when you were a child? Maybe you discovered its power when you used it to focus a ray of sunlight. (I wonder how many insects have been burned to a crisp on sidewalks and driveways?) Even if you weren't mischievous, you soon realized how that small oval piece of glass could transform the words in a comic book. Simply holding the magnifying glass above the page made those little letters become BIG.

The psalm writer says over and over again that the Lord is great. That is His way to describe the immeasurable qualities of the Lord of the universe. Obviously, one five-letter word is not nearly adequate to support the weight of God's glory. But it provides us with a magnifying glass of sorts with which to examine His goodness and enlarge His worth (at least in our eyes). When we see God's greatness, we realize that He alone is worthy of glory and praise. That's what happens when we take the time to focus on the Lord. He doesn't get any bigger than He already is. But from our perspective, He is greater still. Lift up your voice—great is your Lord!

Great is the LORD and most worthy of praise; his greatness no one can fathom. One generation will commend your works to another; they will tell of your mighty acts.

PSALM 145:3, 4

PRAYER

Pray with your eyes wide open. In fact, hold a magnifying glass over Psalm 145 and pray the words of the psalmist aloud. Allow the larger-than-normal letters to boost your confidence in the Lord's worthiness.

D A Y   7

W E   G I V E   T H A N K S

We give thanks to You, O Lord, Almighty God—
The One who is, who was, and is to come.
You've taken up Your power and begun to reign;
The nations bow before the Holy One.

—MARK ALTROGGE

ithin a couple months of the September 11th terrorist attacks on the World Trade Center and the Pentagon, United States troops defeated Taliban strongholds. For the first time in decades, Afghan women were allowed to appear in public without having their faces covered. The return of the government to the people of Afghanistan represented a milepost of victory. But the war on terrorism would require additional offensive operations.

Similarly, followers of Christ live between the inauguration and the culmination of His rule. When Jesus came to earth, He staked the boundaries of the kingdom of God. But what He announced through His teaching and validated by His death and resurrection are not complete. The initial and crucial battle has been waged. The deceiver of our souls has been dealt a fatal blow, and his doom is certain. But the kingdom has not been fully established. The Father, in His time and according to His purposes, will complete the victory. The Son will return to reign in power. Meanwhile, we have reason to give thanks. Lift your voice in a joyful song. After all, the battle is the Lord's. One day, all nations will bow to Him. Read the last chapter of His book. We win!

"I am the Alpha and the Omega," says the Lord God, "who is, and who was, and who is to come, the Almighty."

REVELATION 1:8

PRAYER

Pray for those who have been victimized by evil. Ask the Lord to draw near to them with His mercy and compassion. Thank Him that the justice consistent with His holiness and love will eventually come to pass.

I W I L L B L E S S T H E L O R D

I will bless the Lord and give Him glory;
I will bless His name and give Him glory.

I will bless You, Lord, and give You glory;
I will bless Your name and give You glory.

—FRANK HERNANDEZ

h-choo! When someone sneezes in your presence, what do you say? You either say, "Guzundheit!" or you say, "God bless you!" And for good reason. For a brief moment, a sneeze has interrupted a person's heartbeat. The mindless response that we automatically say is actually a prayer for God to care for the person.

The dictionary definition of "bless" is to consecrate, sanctify, or bestow divine favor upon something or someone. We ask God to bless our homes. We ask Him to bless our nation. We can also entreat the Father to bless our children.

Have you ever wondered why we say, "Bless the Lord?" How are we capable of blessing the Lord? Now there's a conundrum. But wait! If the Lord blesses us (and He does), then when we are called to bless Him (which we are), it means that we are invited to return the compliment. With words, attitudes, behavior, and songs on our lips, we willingly reflect back His goodness as a way to honor His greatness. In other words, we are showering our Creator with adoration and gratitude. So go ahead, let everything you do and say bless His holy name.

Enter his gates with thanksgiving; go into his courts with praise. Give thanks to him and bless his name.

PSALM 100:4 (NLT)

PRAYER

Tell the Lord that you want to bless Him—that is, you desire to reflect back to Him the blessings He has so generously given you. Then ask Him to show you how to do it.

17

I   W I L L   M A G N I F Y

For You are King of kings

And Lord of lords

And You reign in majesty,

Omnipotent Father,

Creator of all things.

I will magnify Your name, O Lord;

I will exalt You forevermore!

—RUSSELL LOWE

o, I don't want to spend eternity in heaven!" The fourteen-year-old girl's emphatic words surprised her pastor-father. "Yes, I know Jesus will be there and I want to see Him, but I can't get all that excited about floating on a cloud plucking a harp!"

For a teenager on the verge of adulthood, spending forever singing the same songs over and over sounded boring. The problem for this young woman was her definition of heaven. Nowhere in Scripture is eternity painted with such mundane colors.

According to the Book of Revelation (where we get our most descriptive, albeit symbolic, picture of heaven), a lot of activity goes on in the presence of the Lord. And what's more, we are told that the King of kings and Lord of lords will be reigning. Have you ever heard of a monarch reigning where the subjects are allowed to just sit around? Not on your life! And not in your afterlife either! There will be so much wonder, beauty, and meaning to our existence that we will find ourselves exulting in our identity as the bride of Christ and willingly exalting Him in all that we will be doing.

I heard a loud shout from the throne, saying, "Look, the home of God is now among his people! He will live with them, and they will be his people. God himself will be with them."

REVELATION 21:3 (NLT)

PRAYER

Meditate on the concept of being with Jesus eternally in heaven. Thank Him that although you don't comprehend it all, you can be sure you will be there, ready to do whatever the King desires!

I B E L I E V E I N J E S U S

I believe in Jesus.
I believe He is the Son of God.
I believe He died and rose again.
I believe He paid for us all.

And I believe He's here now,
Standing in our midst,
Here with the power to heal now
And the grace to forgive.

—MARC NELSON

n old spiritual asks, "Were you there when they crucified my Lord?" Obviously, we can't answer a literal yes. The Savior died two millennia ago. Those who were there, standing at the foot of that blood-stained cross, included disciples, soldiers, and passersby. They saw more than they could fully understand. The sinless Son of God was subjected to cruel punishment and a heinous execution. But the true injustice was the fact that Jesus took on Himself the shame and guilt of all sin of all time.

Before He died, those who stood around heard Him say, "It is finished" (John 19:30). Curiously, in the language Jesus spoke, what He actually said could be translated, "Paid in full!" In other words, Jesus allowed our moral debt of holiness to be paid in full by Him. By His sinless life and sacrificial death, Jesus was willing to foot the bill.

Then to prove He had the moral reserves to actually cover what He offered to pay for, He defeated death. Because of the resurrection, Jesus is standing in our midst. Next time you reach for your credit card or checkbook, thank God that you are covered when it comes to financing your eternity.

God has purchased our freedom with his blood and has forgiven all our sins.

COLOSSIANS 1:14 (NLT)

PRAYER

Express your gratitude to the Lord for His unmerited mercy in your life. Ask Him to soften your heart to the gift of salvation that is so easily taken for granted. Ask His help to forgive those who have offended you in light of the debt He has paid in your life.

WE BRING THE SACRIFICE OF PRAISE

We bring the sacrifice of praise
Into the house of the Lord.
We bring the sacrifice of praise
Into the house of the Lord.
And we offer up to You
The sacrifices of thanksgiving.
And we offer up to You
The sacrifices of joy.

—KIRK DEARMAN

id you get anything out of church today?" the critical husband asked his wife as they drove to their favorite diner for Sunday dinner. "I kept waiting to hear something I could take with me that would last me through the week," he continued.

Sadly, that comment is heard in many cars between the church and Sunday lunch. In many situations, the sermon or the service has not been planned so that worshipers have a sense of what they are to do in light of what they've sung, prayed, or heard.

But no matter how lacking a sermon or service might be, the pastor and worship leader are not entirely to blame. When we enter the sanctuary on Sunday morning, we cannot expect simply to take. By definition, those who come to worship have something to give. To worship means to "offer worth" to the object of their worship. We have the responsibility to offer the sacrifice of praise. We may not leave church having gotten much out of it, but the question we need to ask ourselves is this: In our singing, praying, listening, and thinking, did we offer the Lord a gift? What did *He* get out of the service?

Through Jesus, therefore, let us continually offer to God a sacrifice of praise the fruit of lips that confess his name. And do not forget to do good and to share with others, for with such sacrifices God is pleased.

HEBREWS 13:15, 16

PRAYER

Before you ask God for anything in your prayer time today, spend some extended time reminding Him (and yourself) how faithful and good He has been to you. Write down ten reasons that He is worthy of your praise.

SING HALLELUJAH TO THE LORD!

Sing hallelujah to the Lord!
Sing hallelujah to the Lord!
Sing hallelujah, sing hallelujah,
Sing hallelujah to the Lord!

—LINDA STASSEN-BENJAMIN

any songs include the word "hallelujah" in the lyrics.

Centuries before the birth of Christ, songs were composed that incorporated that hauntingly beautiful Hebrew word that simply means "praise God." Before David ascended Israel's throne, he penned hymns of praise. Exiled Jews in Babylon sang "hallelujah" to the Lord as they called on Him for deliverance. They sang that familiar word when, at long last, they made their pilgrimage back to Jerusalem.

And then there were the disciples of Jesus who, upon realizing the One raised from the dead was indeed the promised Messiah, recast the ancient word to praise the Lamb of God. From the first century on, psalms, hymns, and spiritual songs are generously punctuated with "hallelujah." It was no accident that George Frederic Handel included the "Hallelujah Chorus" in his immortal oratorio *Messiah*. He had to. No retelling of the life of Jesus or the rehearsal of God's faithfulness in history to His people could avoid it. Through the years it has become a universal word. The same in any language. And the language of worship is incomplete without it. No wonder it will be part of heaven's vocabulary. Allow "hallelujah" to fall from your lips multiple times today.

Then I heard what sounded like a great multitude, like the roar of rushing waters and like loud peals of thunder, shouting: "Hallelujah! For our Lord God Almighty reigns."

REVELATION 19:6

PRAYER

No need for many words today. As you go to prayer, slowly repeat "hallelujah" over and over again. Vary your volume. Speak this wonderful word with expression.

K I N G   O F   K I N G S

King of kings and Lord of lords,
Glory hallelujah!
King of kings and Lord of lords,
Glory hallelujah!
Jesus, Prince of Peace,
Glory hallelujah!
Jesus, Prince of Peace,
Glory hallelujah!

—SOPHIE CONY AND NOMI YAH

n a hot summer day in the Middle East, a twelve-year-old boy climbs an olive tree in the courtyard near his home. In the distance, above the sound of bleating sheep, he hears a quiet cadence of drums. He climbs higher in the tree. Straining his eyes, he sees a parade of people on the horizon.

Leading the way is a solitary figure. He is naked except for a loincloth. And he is dancing. The people who follow on his heels are obviously happy. As the throng draws closer to town, the boy can hear the sounds of singing. And then he sees it: a golden box hoisted on parallel poles, carried by men in royal garb. Following in step, two men hold high a royal banner. The banner bears King David's insignia. The man at the front of the procession is the king, leading the ark of the covenant back to Jerusalem like a child dancing before the King of all kings.

If you had been that child, chances are your heart would have pounded with excitement as you listened to the tambourine chatter and the people sing. Fortunately, worship of the same King is still possible today.

David, wearing a linen ephod, danced before the LORD with all his might, while he and the entire house of Israel brought up the ark of the LORD with shouts and the sound of trumpets.

2 SAMUEL 6:14, 15

PRAYER

The Lord is indeed King of all kings and Lord of lords. Imagine what that means. As you approach Him in prayer, remind yourself that He is able to do anything. All authority and dominion are His.

27

GLORY

Glory, glory in the highest;
Glory to the Almighty.
Glory to the Lamb of God,
And glory to the Living Word.
Glory to the Lamb!

—DANNY DANIELS

or more than 200 years Americans have referred to their flag as "Old Glory"—and for good reason. The red, white, and blue recalls the days of glory when courageous soldiers fought to save the footings of democracy that had only recently been poured. They were glorious days indeed. So when our flag flutters overhead, illuminated by the late afternoon sun, patriotic hearts mark double time.

But the glory we speak of when referring to the Most High God is of another kind. It is not stirring memories of yesteryear. It is hardly patriotism or pride. The glorious majesty that surrounds heaven's throne invites our wonder and awe. Like a magnet, it draws from the depths of our hearts exuberant adoration as well as hushed reverence. This glory is not a nation's flag. It is the banner of praise that flies from deep within hearts that are aware of the One who has washed them clean.

Thus, the glory of God is that which radiates from His invisible yet holy presence. But it is also what is due Him. To that end, give Him the glory He deserves by reminding yourself today that you are a citizen of the kingdom of heaven.

Praise be to the LORD God, the God of Israel, who alone does marvelous deeds. Praise be to his glorious name forever; may the whole earth be filled with his glory. Amen and Amen.

PSALM 72:18, 19

PRAYER

As an offering of praise, think of the word "glory" as an acronym. Come up with words that ascribe worth to God that begin with each of those five letters (for example, Gracious, Loving, Ordering, Righteous, Yielding).

I WILL SING OF THE MERCIES OF THE LORD

I will sing of the mercies
Of the Lord forever.
I will sing, I will sing,
I will sing of the mercies
Of the Lord forever.
I will sing of the mercies of the Lord.

—JAMES H. FILLMORE

W
hen Gunder Birkeland whistled a tune, his wife and children knew he wasn't feeling well. That was his unique way of dealing with chronic pain. As a child, Gunder contracted polio and succumbed to the crippling powers of the disease that left his feet twisted, his back hunched, and his body wracked with pain. Although Gunder learned how to cope with constant discomfort, some days were just plain hard. On those days, he whistled.

As he grew up, Gunder discovered the unconditional acceptance of a loving God. He learned that a forgiven heart was far more important than an attractive physique or a pain-free life. Once he trusted Christ as his Savior, Gunder began to recognize the many blessings a day could bring. He credited the Lord with profitable business deals, wisdom to raise three kids, and the desire to reach out to those who struggled with health issues like he had. Mercies, Gunder called them. God's undeserved mercies.

Something else Gunder did signaled how grateful he was for God's many blessings. He sang—not very well mind you. He couldn't carry a tune five feet. But that shriveled little body contained a huge heart that couldn't contain God's love without lifting his voice in praise.

As you know, we consider blessed those who have persevered. You have heard of Job's perseverance and have seen what the LORD finally brought about. The Lord is full of compassion and mercy.

JAMES 5:11

PRAYER

Thank the Lord for ways He has been merciful to you in the last twelve months. Be as specific as you can. Then sing of the mercies of the Lord with a song of praise—and it doesn't matter how well you can sing!

A N C I E N T O F D A Y S

Blessing and honor, glory and power
Be unto the Ancient of Days.
From every nation all of creation
Bow before the Ancient of Days.

Every tongue in Heaven and earth
Shall declare Your glory.
Every knee shall bow at Your throne in worship.
You will be exalted, oh God,
And Your kingdom shall not pass away,
O Ancient of Days.

—JAMIE HARVILL AND GARY SADLER

f all the names for God, Ancient of Days is probably the most obscure. It's a name that sounds as old as the hills or as ancient as ancient history. And that is exactly what this reference to the Lord is supposed to imply. It calls to mind the reality of the preexistence of the Creator. Just try and fathom it. Before time began, God had been on the scene for millions of years. But no one was counting.

The six days of Creation are difficult enough to grasp without attempting to step behind the curtain of time in hopes of finding the stage manager of the cosmos. No matter. We wouldn't be able to see Him anyway. The Ancient of Days cannot be seen with the human eye. Yet one day, all will see Him and bow down to worship Him.

Although God can't be understood, take comfort in knowing that beyond just willing your life into being, He wills to have a relationship with you. Now that's a truth you can take to the bank. It's a desire in the heart of God that predates Adam and Eve, but it's as current as this very day.

At the name of Jesus every knee should bow, in heaven and on earth and under the earth, and every tongue confess that Jesus Christ is Lord, to the glory of God the Father.

PHILIPPIANS 2:10, 11

PRAYER

Confess your finite understanding to One who understands the end from the beginning. If you are struggling with an overwhelming issue that is beyond your control, candidly express your concerns to the Lord. Turn them over to Him.

O U R   G O D   I S   L I F T E D   U P

Our God is lifted up
Midst the shouts of joy.
Our God is lifted up
In the sounding of the trumpets.
Our God is lifted up
Midst the shouts of joy.
Shout joyfully unto our God!
Shout joyfully unto our God!

—TIM SMITH

rom time immemorial, worship has been characterized by more than singing. In the days of the Old Testament, the people of God came before Him with chants and shouts. They paraded in the presence of the Most High with all kinds of instruments: flutes, lyres, harps, drums, trumpets, cymbals, tambourines. This included rhythmic movements—the lyrics of praise called for both verbal and body language. Championing the cause of God can't be accomplished by offering passive approval for what He has done.

If you've ever been to a championship college football game, you've felt the electricity of emotion. When the clock has elapsed and one team has won, the band lets loose with the school's fight song. The cheerleading squad bids all spectators become participants in the victory celebration. The players, having doused their coach with a ten-gallon container of icy water, proceed to lift him up on their shoulders and parade him onto the gridiron.

Although our worship celebrations are more controlled and sane than the frenzy of a football game, we have much to learn from those occasions. Lifting up the Lord requires more than lifting up a hymnbook. Let your singing be like joyful shouts to your Lord!

Praise him with the sounding of the trumpet, praise him with the harp and lyre, praise him with tambourine and dancing, praise him with the strings and flute, praise him with the clash of cymbals, praise him with resounding cymbals.

PSALM 150:3-5

PRAYER

Spend time imagining yourself in a setting where Psalm 150 was being acted out. Ask the Lord to help you sing with great joy, lifting up and glorifying Him.

L E T   T H E R E   B E   G L O R Y   A N D   H O N O R   A N D   P R A I S E S

Let there be glory and honor and praises—
Glory and honor to Jesus,
Glory and honor,
Glory and honor to Him.

—James and Elizabeth Greenelsh

f you're old enough, you may remember that song The Byrds sang in the sixties: "For every thing, turn, turn, turn. There is a season, turn, turn, turn." Their lyrics came right out of Ecclesiastes, chapter 3. There is "a time to cry and a time to laugh. A time to grieve and a time to dance" (Ecclesiastes 3:4).

So what is the appropriate attitude for Sunday morning worship? Is there a time to laugh, as well as a time to cry? A time to grieve as well as a time to dance? Should we come into the presence of the Lord with thinking minds or throbbing hearts? Would you believe—both?

Jesus said we are to worship Him in spirit and truth (John 4:23). In other words, we don't have to arbitrarily choose. It's not "either, or" but "both, and." A sane, thoughtful, and prayerful encounter with the living God brings a smile to His face. But so does a passionate rehearsal of His faithfulness expressed with the emotional faculties He created in us.

Simply put, worship requires both honor and glory. The key is being alert to what seems appropriate and then responding accordingly.

Yet a time is coming and has now come when the true worshipers will worship the Father in spirit and truth, for they are the kind of worshipers the Father seeks.

JOHN 4:23

PRAYER

Pray for your pastor and worship leaders. Ask God to give them an ability to appropriately balance the necessary elements as they plan congregational worship.

WE WILL DANCE

We will dance
On the streets that are golden.
The glorious bride
And the great Son of Man.
From every tongue
And tribe and nation, we'll join
In the song of the Lamb.

—DAVID RUIS

hat do you like most about going to a wedding? (I mean other than the frosting-laden cake and salted nuts at the reception.) Most likely it is the atmosphere of joy and beauty that defies description. Like they say, you've never seen an ugly bride. If the wedding is of someone you know well, your interest is elevated.

The occasion is far from ordinary. The music is carefully chosen and well rehearsed. Families, often separated by distance, are reunited. Vows of committed love are shared. God's counsel for marital success is offered by a robed cleric. Tokens of affection are exchanged. The congregation arrives appropriately attired and bearing costly gifts. And at many weddings the reception includes more than cake and nuts or coffee and mints. There might just be a sit-down dinner and . . . dancing!

No wonder the Bible pictures heaven as the union of Christ and His bride. It's a place of love, joy, music, laughter, reconciliation, long-overdue justice, and togetherness. Scripture calls attention to the marriage supper of the Lamb. The atmosphere will be thick with the presence of God Himself. No red carpet runner will do. Streets paved with pure gold, please! And would you believe even the "non-dancers" will dance?

Then the angel said to me, "Write: 'Blessed are those who are invited to the wedding supper of the Lamb!'" And he added, "These are the true words of God."

REVELATION 19:9

PRAYER

Get out your wedding album and review it in an attitude of prayer. Ask the Lord to intervene in areas of your marriage where you are currently struggling. But don't stop there. Ask the Lord to fill your heart with an increasing homesickness for heaven.

W O R T H Y ,   Y O U   A R E   W O R T H Y

Worthy, You are worthy.

King of kings, Lord of lords,

You are worthy.

Worthy, You are worthy.

King of kings, Lord of lords,

I worship You.

—DON MOEN

esus is worthy of our praise. The sooner we learn that, the sooner we will stop our busy-ness to sit in His presence, as Mary of Bethany did so long ago.

The story recorded in Luke 10:38–42 describes Jesus paying Mary and Martha a visit. Martha was stressed out about getting a meal on the table. Her sister Mary, however, was sitting at the Savior's feet, feasting on His every word. Martha asked Jesus to insist that Mary give her some help. But Jesus did not comply with her request, and the reason was clear. He wanted to teach Martha a lesson. He wanted the older sister to learn that there is more to life than the art of entertaining or a fixation with food. What Jesus saw in Mary was a portrait He wanted to hold up as an example of how to set proper priorities.

Mary had recognized that her friend from Nazareth was more than a carpenter. He was more than a rabbi. He was the long-awaited Messiah. He was worthy of her worship. He is worthy of our attention. He is worthy of letting all else wait. Don't neglect time in His presence today.

I call to the LORD, who is worthy of praise.

2 SAMUEL 22:4

PRAYER

Confess to the Lord your tendency to obsess over insignificant details that derail your devotion to Him. Spend quiet time in His presence.

A S H I E L D A B O U T M E

Thou, O Lord,

Art a shield about me.

You're my glory;

You're the lifter of my head.

Thou, O Lord,

Art a shield about me.

You're my glory

And the lifter of my head.

—DONN THOMAS AND CHARLES WILLIAMS

ohnny hadn't meant to hurt anyone, least of all the family dog, Bruno. When the ten-year-old had unwrapped his last birthday present, he was so excited he just had to try it out. He had asked for a BB gun for his Christmas and his birthday for the last three years. But up till now, his parents thought him too young. Johnny raced into the wheat fields in back of the farmhouse and began shooting his new toy. He hadn't realized Bruno had run after him and ran right in line of the metal pellets. The dog had been badly hurt.

Johnny moped around the house unable to look anyone in the eye. But after several hours, his wise father sat beside his son and lifted his chin with his hand. "I know you are sorry for what happened," he said gently. "We all have forgiven you. It's time you forgave yourself."

Like Johnny, we know what it's like to be sorry for our sins. But too often we live with unnecessary regret and guilt. The Father desires to lift our heads and remind us we are fully forgiven. Why don't you let Him today?

But thou, O LORD, art a shield for me; my glory, and the lifter up of mine head.

PSALM 3:3 (KJV)

PRAYER

Picture yourself kneeling before the King of kings who is seated on His holy throne. Visualize the Lord reaching down and lifting up your bowed head. Hear him say to you, "My child, because I love you, forgive yourself."

F I N D   U S   F A I T H F U L

Oh, may all who come behind us find us
faithful.
May the fire of our devotion light their
way.
May the footprints that we leave lead
them to believe
And the lives we live inspire them to
obey.
Oh, may all who come behind us find us
faithful.

—JOHN MOHR

lfred Nobel, after whom the Nobel Peace Prize is named, was originally known for his invention of a substance that nations would utilize in war. Nobel, a Swedish-born scientist, invented dynamite. How he decided to channel his energies in a more positive direction is a curious story.

It seems Nobel was sipping his morning coffee while reading the newspaper. As he turned to the obituaries to read what was said about his recently deceased brother, he was shocked to see his own name. The newspaper had inadvertently published Alfred's name instead of his brother's. What was a further shock to the great scientist was seeing that if he had died, all the world would remember him for was "the invention of a deadly explosive." At that point, Nobel decided he would use his fortune to reward those who would dedicate their lives to the furtherance of peace. As a result of that decision, Alfred Nobel revised his own legacy.

How do you want to be remembered? As a success in your vocational field? As one who achieved great wealth? Or as one who successfully passed the baton of faith to those whom you had the opportunity to influence?

I have been reminded of your sincere faith, which first lived in your grandmother Lois and in your mother Eunice and, I am persuaded, now lives in you also.

2 TIMOTHY 1:5

PRAYER

Think about those who left a faithful witness in the world and passed the baton of faith to you. Thank the Lord for their influence in your life. Ask the Lord to use you in the same way in the lives of those who come behind you.

H O W   B E A U T I F U L

How beautiful the hands that served
The wine and the bread to the sons of the earth.
How beautiful the feet that walked
The long dusty roads and the hill to the Cross.
How beautiful, how beautiful, how beautiful is
the Body of Christ.

—TWILA PARIS

hirley's hands weren't pretty at all. They were calloused and wrinkled. She had worked hard for most of her sixty years. Raising three energetic children had taken its toll, as had her hands-on responsibility in the family trucking business. But Shirley's hands were not too weary to serve the Lord. Her hands gladly went to work for the body of Christ.

When Shirley was asked one Friday to bake bread for Sunday's celebration of the Lord's Supper, those same hands went to work willingly. The next month when the pastor asked if she would prepare the elements for Communion, she excitedly agreed. With joy she poured grape juice and broke her homemade loaf into bite-sized morsels. In fact, Shirley asked if she could serve the Lord in that special way each month. For years thereafter Shirley's "beautiful" hands set the table for God's people. It was obvious she had firmly grasped what Jesus had modeled—humbly laying down her life by giving what she had to offer for the sake of Christ's church. What is it that the Lord would like your hands to do for the body of Christ? Your hands don't need to be "beautiful," they just need to be available.

And since I, the Lord and Teacher, have washed your feet, you ought to wash each other's feet. I have given you an example to follow. Do as I have done to you.

JOHN 13:14, 15 (NLT)

PRAYER

Today as you go to prayer, don't fold your hands. Open them as a gesture of availability. Confess to the Lord ways you've held back serving His church. Determine to use the gifts God has given you in ministry to others.

T H I S   I S   T H E   D A Y

This is the day
That the Lord has made.
I will rejoice
And be glad in it.
O this is the day
That the Lord has made;
I will rejoice
And be glad in it.

Rejoice in the Lord, rejoice in the Lord.
Celebrate the presence of the Lord,
For He is worthy to be praised.

—RICK SHELTON/LES GARRETT

s Olga Birkeland grew older, the arteries in her brain became restricted. Blood flow was limited, and her capacity of mental recall was impacted. Her family grieved the gradual loss of the mother and grandmother who had been the life of the party. Against the dark backdrop of the dreaded disease that stole Olga's memory, however, there shone a bright spot.

No matter what day of the week it was, this sweet Christian woman insisted that it was Sunday. "Today is Sunday and that means we're going to church!" she would say. "Aren't you going to get dressed? We don't want to be late." The profound experiences in worship that Olga had known earlier in her life had engraved themselves on the tissues of her brain. Somewhere deep in her failing mind, she wanted it to always be Sunday.

In a way, Olga Birkeland was right. For the Christian, every day is the Lord's Day. Each morning announces His promise of His presence, complete with grace and mercy. Since each day is one that the Lord has made, we have every reason to anticipate something wonderful.

Rejoice in this day that God has made and has given to you!

This is the day the LORD has made; we will rejoice and be glad in it.

PSALM 118:24 (NKJV)

PRAYER

Instead of praying your typical prayer, make a "to do" list for what you need to accomplish today. As you write down each item, commit it to the Lord and ask His help.

N E W   E V E R Y   M O R N I N G

The Lord's lovingkindnesses indeed will
never cease,
And His compassions will never fade away.
They are new every morning;
They are new every day,
For great is Thy faithfulness.

The Lord's amazing grace—
It abounds to us every day,
And His great mercies will never fade away.
They are new every morning;
They are new every day,
For great is Thy faithfulness,
For great is Thy faithfulness.

—Scott Underwood

o ahead. Picture yourself in South Texas at a Christian dude ranch. Needing a change of pace, you've come to the right place. The work that you will be doing all day is backbreaking and draining. But as you work alongside real-life cowhands, you find yourself grateful for a body that functions as God created it. This work is so different than what you're accustomed to, it almost seems like recreation.

Later, with other campers, you join the staff around a blazing campfire. The crackling logs explode, shooting sparks skyward. As you look overhead, you see what appear to be millions of crushed diamonds against black velvet. Someone strums a guitar; another picks up a harmonica. Before long, an unrobed choir of untrained voices breaks forth in praise to God for another day of grace. You sing along with all your heart because you are mindful of daily mercies like never before. It's a little piece of heaven on earth.

Now, take that same attitude toward life and God's gracious provision and live it today, in your home, neighborhood, and work. Indeed, this *is* the day that the Lord has made—so rejoice and be glad!

Because of the LORD's great love we are not consumed, for his compassions never fail. They are new every morning; great is your faithfulness.

LAMENTATIONS 3:22, 23

PRAYER

As you find your favorite chair to spend some time in prayer, take along a blank sheet of paper. Contemplate the gift of an unblemished new day that promises new evidence of the Lord's mercies.

H O L Y   L O V E

Many waters cannot quench Your love
Rivers cannot overwhelm it,
Oceans of fear cannot conceal
Your love for me.

Holy love flow in me
Fill me up like the deepest sea,
Like a crashing wave
Pouring over me
Holy love flow in me.

When I find You I find healing,
When I find You I find peace,
And I know that there's no river so wide
No mountain so high, no ocean so deep
That You can't part the sea.

—ANDY PARK

he Oregon Coast is a thing of beauty. The craggy rocks that define the shoreline are quite a contrast from the smooth sandy beaches of California. But the long, rugged shoreline of the Northwest boasts romance and personality. The blue waters of the Pacific drench mile after mile of tidewaters in which grow tall evergreen trees. The approaching waves fall like the pages of a book blown by an unexpected breeze.

Anyone who has spent time beachcombing along Reedsport, Florence, or Lincoln City knows that what is lovely and beautiful to look at is at the same time a power to be reckoned with. Lives are lost each year off the Oregon Coast by those who failed to respect the mysterious force that churns beneath the tranquil glass-like sea.

The Lord is at once loving and holy. He is not to be taken lightly or dismissed as sentimental. That His love is beautiful to behold (not to mention life-changing when embraced) cannot be disputed. But His is a *holy* love that demands reverence and awe. When we come to Him aware of who He is, we can drink in the unequalled splendor of the Almighty God who has demonstrated His never-ending love that is deeper than the deepest sea.

The mighty oceans have roared, O LORD. The mighty oceans roar like thunder; the mighty oceans roar as they pound the shore. But mightier than the violent raging of the seas, mightier than the breakers on the shore—the LORD above is mightier than these!

PSALM 93:3, 4 (NLT)

PRAYER

No words need be spoken in the Lord's presence today. Simply linger in reverent silence aware of the ocean-like power of His holy love.

C O M E   A N D   F I L L   M E   U P

I can feel You flowin' through me;
Holy Spirit, come and fill me up.
Come and fill me up.
Love and mercy fill my senses;
I am thirsty for Your presence, Lord;
Come and fill me up.

Lord, let Your mercy
Wash away all of my sin.
Fill me completely
With Your love once again.
I need You, I want You,
I love Your presence.

—CRAIG MUSSEAU

ou may not feel thirsty, but you need to be drinking all the time." The tour guide smiled as he gave his warning. But it was obvious to the group of tourists in Israel that he was serious. Because they had never toured the Middle East before, they listened carefully.

The guide continued, "Because of the intense summer sun, your body loses more fluid that you realize through perspiration. Don't simply drink when you are thirsty. Keep sipping throughout the day. If you don't, you'll begin to dehydrate."

At times, we open the Bible desiring to drink in the Lord's presence. During those moments, the Lord seems close, and we can't ignore our thirst for more of Him. On other occasions, however, the thought of spending time with the Father seems like an obligation or an interruption in our routine. We don't feel thirsty for the Living Water. Any seasoned traveler on the path of faith would warn us that we need to "drink" all the time—whether we "feel" thirsty or not. Life saps us of what we can only find in the Lord's presence.

Make sure that you take time to irrigate your soul today.

O God, you are my God, earnestly I seek you; my soul thirsts for you, my body longs for you, in a dry and weary land where there is no water.

PSALM 63:1

PRAYER

In addition to your regular time of personal worship, stop and pray each time you take a coffee break today. As you take a sip, allow the Lord to swallow up the little worries that have plagued your mind.

THE POWER OF YOUR LOVE

Lord, I come to You;

Let my heart be changed, renewed,

Flowing from the grace that I found in You.

Lord, I've come to know

The weaknesses I see in me

Will be stripped away by the power of Your love.

Hold me close;

Let Your love surround me.

Bring me near; draw me to Your side.

And as I wait,

I'll rise up like the eagle,

And I will soar with You.

Your Spirit leads me on

in the power of Your love.

—GEOFF BULLOCK

ome, Alaska, came to prominence during the days of the Yukon Gold Rush. Today it is primarily known as the terminus of the Iditarod sled dog race. This little town of three thousand people is situated on the Bering Sea and perched on the permafrost that the Native Americans of the north call "tundra."

If you've been in Nome in both the summer and the winter, you might think you are in two different towns. During the summer, the muddy dirt roads in front of wood-frame houses are littered with abandoned cars, rusted-out washing machines, and broken furniture. Once the snows come, the garbage-strewn town is a virtual fairyland. A blanket of white covers all the unsightly litter. But, as you might expect, when the spring thaw comes, reality returns.

Except for the power of God's redeeming love, our lives would be much like Nome. From time to time we could successfully cover the ugliness of our guilt and shame, but not for long. What is buried eventually is exposed. What we could not bring about on our own, however, God has done by His amazing grace. He has replaced our garbage with His goodness.

The power of God's love has made you clean—completely clean.

"Come now, let us argue this out," says the LORD. "No matter how deep the stain of your sins, I can remove it. I can make you as clean as freshly fallen snow. Even if you are stained as red as crimson, I can make you as white as wool."

ISAIAH 1:18 (NLT)

PRAYER

Ask the Lord to change and renew your heart. Ask Him to strip away your weaknesses and deal with your sins by the power of His great love.

A M A Z I N G   L O V E

My Lord, what love is this
That pays so dearly
That I, the guilty one, may go free?

Amazing love! O what sacrifice—
The Son of God given for me.
My debt He pays, and my death He dies
That I might live, that I might live.

And so they watched Him die,
Despised, rejected.
But O, the blood He shed flowed for me.
And now this love of Christ
Shall flow like rivers;
Come, wash your guilt away; live again.

—GRAHAM KENDRICK

aybe you have seen that stunning painting that depicts Christ's amazing love. A person stands behind a dark-haired man who is no longer strong enough to stand on his own. But it's not just anybody who is bearing him up with strong embracing arms. It's Jesus!

Upon closer examination, you see the details in this portrait of love. The man being held by the Lord is stained with blood. In his limp hand, he still grasps a hammer. From the context of the scene, we are left with the unmistakable impression that Jesus is holding the person responsible for His crucifixion.

But that man with the hammer is more than just the man in the painting. He represents each of us. Although the Roman soldiers were the ones who drove spikes into Jesus' wrists, they acted on our behalf. *Our* sin caused Jesus to be tortured and to die. Indirectly, *we* nailed Him to the cross. Yet, guilty as we are, Jesus comes behind us and holds up. Talk about amazing love. That's exactly what it is.

When confronted by the reality of God's amazing love for you, how do you feel? How can you respond?

This is real love. It is not that we loved God, but that he loved us and sent his Son as a sacrifice to take away our sins.

1 JOHN 4:10 (NLT)

PRAYER

Picture yourself in that famous painting. Feel the arms of Jesus holding you up. Release your sense of guilt in shame and allow them to fall at your feet . . . and His.

D R A W   M E   C L O S E

Draw me close to You; never let me go.
I lay it all down again to hear You say
That I'm Your friend.
You are my desire; no one else will do,
'Cause nothing else could take your place,
To feel the warmth of Your embrace.
Help me find the way;
Bring me back to You.

You're all I want;
You're all I've ever needed.
You're all I want;
Help me know You are near.

—KELLY CARPENTER

he Bible has many stories about blind people being healed by Jesus. Perhaps the most dramatic, however, is that of Bartimaeus. As this blind beggar sits by the side of the road, his hope is nearly gone. Jericho's famed groves of trees provide shade for the sightless man, but nothing can shield him from the sense of worthlessness and shame.

One day as the townsfolk chatter amid their typical routines, Bartimaeus hears talk that arrests his attention. The miracle-working rabbi from Galilee is approaching the village. He has heard of the amazing feats this carpenter-turned-teacher has performed. In his lonely heart he dares to wonder if Jesus might have the power to heal him.

No doubt you know the rest of the story. As Jesus draws close, Bartimaeus cries out, "Jesus, Son of David, have mercy on me!" (Mark 10:47). Even though the crowd tries to silence the beggar, he cries out all the more. Blind Bartimaeus was so needy, he had nothing to lose. He longed to be drawn close to the Lord with the cords of love. And Jesus did not disappoint him.

What disables your faith today? Call out to this same Jesus and let Him draw you to Himself.

Then I pray to you, O LORD. I say, "You are my place of refuge. You are all I really want in life."

PSALM 142:5 (NLT)

PRAYER

Take your cue from Bartimaeus. Sit cross-legged on the floor and close your eyes. Admit your need to the Lord and reach out your arms. Call out to Him by name.

J E S U S ,   W H A T   A
W O N D E R   Y O U   A R E !

Jesus, what a wonder You are!
You are so gentle, so pure and so kind,
You shine like the morning star.
Jesus, what a wonder You are!

—DAVE BOLTON

arly one Sunday, Pastor Troy left for church with his young family. As he carried his little daughter Lesley to the car, she spotted a bright star. Pointing with her stubby finger, she shrieked.

"That's a morning star, sweetie," her daddy explained. He then began to sing, "Twinkle, twinkle little star, how I wonder what you are. Up above the world so high, like a diamond in the sky. Twinkle, twinkle little star, how I wonder what you are." Little Lesley slipped her thumb in her mouth and laid her head on her daddy's shoulder. A child's wonder had been acknowledged.

Our first introduction to the subject of stars is not all that scientific. Long before we came to understand their chemical consistency or distance from earth, our parents serenaded us about their wonder. There was no need to fully explain their origins or function in order to appreciate their majesty.

Similarly, we don't need a seminary education to understand the wonder of the one the biblical writers call "the Morning Star." His gentleness, purity, and kindness shine down through history and from the pages of God's Word. Even a child can sense His splendor. But it takes a lifetime (and then some) to wonder about all He is about.

"Jesus, what a wonder You are!"

Show the wonder of your great love, you who save by your right hand those who take refuge in you from their foes.

PSALM 17:7

PRAYER

Step outside late at night or early in the morning and look to the twinkling stars overhead. Allow that silent chorus of praise to stimulate your delight in your Creator's power.

J O Y   O F   M Y   D E S I R E

Joy of my desire, all-consuming fire,
Lord of Glory, Rose of Sharon
Rare and sweet,
You are now my peace,
Comforter and Friend,
Wonderful!
So beautiful
You are to me.

I worship You
In spirit and in truth.
I worship You
In spirit and in truth.
There will never be a friend
As dear to me as You.

—JENNIFER RANDOLPH

athy looked ten years older than the date her birth certificate boasted. Not bad for a forty-year-old woman who had already lived two lifetimes. Starved for love as a kid, she rebelled as a teenager and sought the physical affection of any man whose attention she could attract. She had a baby out of wedlock and then another. In addition to the disgrace of her family, the pressures of raising children on her own took their toll. Kathy turned to alcohol and then drugs. But the buzz and the high never filled her emptiness. She baked pies as a way of supporting herself and her two kids.

One Sunday on a lark, Kathy decided to attend a little country church half a mile down the road. One of her best customers attended there. What this modern-day Samaritan woman found in that place was a whole lot more than she bargained for. She met Jesus. In His embrace of grace her definition of love was rewritten. She had found what she had been looking for.

All around us are women (and men) at some well trying to quench a thirst that can only be satisfied by the unconditional love of the Lord. Be on the lookout for them today. Point them to the One who can satisfy their desire and give them joy.

But the water I give them takes away thirst altogether. It becomes a perpetual spring within them, giving them eternal life.

JOHN 4:14 (NLT)

PRAYER

Ask God to open your eyes (and your heart) to someone who is longing to know the love only He can supply.

IN THE LORD ALONE

In the Lord, the Lord alone,
Are righteousness and strength.
The height and breadth
And length of love are found in Him.

In the Lord, the Lord alone,
Are life and health and peace.
His mercies and His loving kindness
Never cease.

In the Lord, the Lord alone,
Is everything I need.
The Son of Man now reigning high
Will intercede.

—WALT HARRAH

wiss army knives are great tools. In one little device you have a virtual took kit in your pocket. In addition to an all-purpose knife, you have a screwdriver, a bottle opener, a pair of miniature scissors, a corkscrew, and a nail file. With your Swiss army knife at hand, you'll be in a position to whittle your way through all kinds of knotty challenges. You will even be a hero to someone whose eyeglass screw has just come loose.

On a much larger scale, that's what the living Lord desires to be to those who worship Him. In Him we have more than a Creator. We have a Savior, a Healer, a Guide, a Defender, a Father, and a Friend. In Him we have the solution to our frailty and sinfulness. In Him we have a Supreme Judge and Servant Leader. In Him alone we have all we would ever need.

No wonder when Jesus commissioned His followers to go into every corner of the world on His behalf, He only equipped them with the promise that He would be with them.

Wherever you go and whatever you face, Jesus is with you—and He's all you need.

Neither height nor depth, nor anything else in all creation, will be able to separate us from the love of God that is in Christ Jesus our Lord.

ROMANS 8:39

PRAYER

On a slip of paper list the various roles the Lord has played in your life since you surrendered to His rule.

YOU ARE MY GOD

You are my God;
You are my King;
You are my Master, my everything.
You are my Lord—
That's why I sing to You,
"Hallelujah, hallelujah!"

—MACON DELAVAN

n Psalm 22 we are privy to King David's deeply intimate thoughts.

Reading those haunting verses is like looking over his shoulder while he makes an entry in his personal journal. It's obvious that David is in much distress. As far as he is concerned, God is on vacation. "My God, my God, why have you forsaken me?" he cries.

But look again. Even though David feels forsaken by God, he expresses his doubt in prayer. Does that surprise you? This psalm is a prayer to God. Wouldn't you think that if David really felt God was nowhere to be found he wouldn't waste his breath complaining? Not so. There is something in David that causes him to believe that God is still within earshot, even if it seems as though He's gone for good.

After all, David knows this God very well. He's been in a tight spot a time or two before and the Lord has always come through. David's words betray his underlying belief that the Lord is *his* God. For David, this relationship is the fruit of a number of years of walking together.

The Lord is your God as well. And as such, He can handle your honest doubts and fears. Don't be afraid to express to Him your thoughts and feelings.

For he has not despised or disdained the suffering of the afflicted one; he has not hidden his face from him but has listened to his cry for help.

PSALM 22:24

PRAYER

Write a letter to God. Use friendship language. Share your fears and hopes. Go ahead and use stationery. Fold it in an envelope and tuck it in your Bible.

You Have Been Good

O Lord, You have been good;
You have been faithful to all generations.
O Lord, Your steadfast love
And tender mercy
Have been our salvation.

For by Your hand we have been fed,
And by Your Spirit we have been led.

O Lord, Almighty God,
Father unchanging, upright and holy!
O Lord, You have been good;
You have been faithful;
You have been good.

—Twila Paris

ere's a song worth playing over and over again. The more you listen to it, the more you want to sing along. This waltz-like melody invites our hearts to dance. Even without lyrics, this tune in three-quarter time can lift the most downcast spirit. It pulls the drapes away from the window of our hearts and lets the sunlight of God's love shine in.

But the song's poignant words join hands with the memorable melody and together they circle around our worshiping hearts. The lyrics point out that God's faithfulness and goodness from which we have benefited have touched the lives of countless generations before us. They paint a series of word pictures that remind us on the cloudiest of days that ours is a God who cannot withhold His penetrating presence from us.

Martha Stewart, the consummate entertainer/homemaker, is known for her signature expression, "It's a good thing." Well, thanks to Twila Paris, we can claim a signature expression by which we greet the Lord each day: "You have been good, Lord."

You are forgiving and good, O Lord, abounding in love to all who call to you. Hear my prayer, O LORD; listen to my cry for mercy.

PSALM 86:5, 6

PRAYER

Today as you pray, simply say, "Lord, it's a good thing that . . . Then finish the statement with something good that the Lord has done.

THY LOVING KINDNESS

Thy loving kindness is better than life;
Thy loving kindness is better than life.
My lips shall praise Thee;
Thus will I bless Thee.
I will lift up my hands unto Thy name.

I lift my hands up unto Thy name;
I lift my hands up unto Thy name.
My lips shall praise Thee;
Thus will I bless Thee.
I will lift up my hands unto Thy name.

—HUGH MITCHELL

p, Daddy, up!" Kristin reached her arms up in the air. "Hold me, Daddy!" Even without words the two-year-old's desire could have been discerned. But added together, the plea was unmistakable. As far as little Kristin was concerned, being in her father's arms was better than life itself. Loving her dad the way she did, she wanted to nuzzle his neck and kiss his face. He had earned her love because he had earned her trust.

When we chronicle the many ways that God has intervened on our behalf, we have every reason to trust Him as a reliable, loving Father. He has proven Himself over and over again. Sometimes we, like tantrum-prone toddlers, are strong-willed enough to deny His goodness. But when we come to our senses and are willing to be honest, we are forced to admit that His loving kindness is, in fact, better than life.

Next time you are in a praise gathering and those around you extend their arms to heaven in adoration, picture yourself as a young child desiring to held by your Father. Lift your hands unto Him. "Hold me, Daddy. Hold me!"

Because your love is better than life, my lips will glorify you. I will praise you as long as I live and in your name I will lift up my hands.

PSALM 63:3, 4

PRAYER

Before coming before the Lord with your laundry list of personal requests, spend several minutes glorifying Him with your lips.

WE HAVE COME INTO THIS HOUSE

Let's forget about ourselves
And magnify the Lord and worship Him.
Let's forget about ourselves
And magnify the Lord and worship Him.
Let's forget about ourselves
And magnify the Lord and worship Him.
Oh, worship Him—Jesus Christ our Lord.

—BRUCE BALLINGER

here is a legend about a Greek immigrant who walked from Lewiston, Idaho, all the way to Washington, D.C., during World War II. This man dearly loved his adopted country. He was too old to fight, but he wanted to find a way to help pay for freedom. Gus determined he would use his feet and his willpower to raise money for the war effort. He would ask his family and friends to give a penny to the war effort for every mile he walked.

Although the trip took Gus several months, by the time he approached the nation's capital, news of the Greek American had reached the president. He and the First Lady sent word to the weary walker that they would like to have dinner with him in the White House. You can imagine the pride that pounded in Gus's heart as he entered the mansion at 1600 Pennsylvania Avenue. With reverence and joy he respectfully deflected every question the president asked him. He simply wanted to enjoy the ambiance and pay his respects to the leader of the free world.

When we enter the Lord's house, we are to do so with a sense of celebration and respect. Worship is all about God. Our concerns and preference are to take a back pew. Worship is an invitation to forget about ourselves and magnify the Lord.

Speak to one another with psalms, hymns and spiritual songs. Sing and make music in your heart to the Lord, always giving thanks to God the Father for everything, in the name of our Lord Jesus Christ.

EPHESIANS 5:19, 20

PRAYER

When you enter the Lord's house this coming Sunday, focus on forgetting about yourself, magnifying the Lord, and worshiping wholeheartedly.

WHATEVER IS TRUE

Whatever is true, whatever is right,
Whatever is pure, whatever is lovely—
We will fix our thoughts on these things.
Jesus, You're true; Jesus, You're right;
Jesus, You're pure; You are lovely.
We will fix our thoughts on You.

Jesus, who is like You?
Jesus, who is like You?
Who is like You?

—BRIAN DOERKSEN AND CRAIG MUSSEAU

he image is disturbing. A frying pan sits atop a kitchen stove. The announcer's voice says, "This is your brain." Then we see someone crack an egg and empty its contents into the sizzling skillet. Once again the announcer speaks. "This is your brain on drugs!"

Sadly, countless teenagers with incredible potential have scrambled their brains by indulging in mind-altering drugs. But there is no turning back. Once the damage is done, the results are irreversible.

A mind is a terrible thing to waste. But that not only is true with regard to drug abuse; it also has to do with the content we upload into the precious organ God gave to each of us. It is true (sometimes alarmingly so!) that we become what we think about. No wonder the apostle Paul was so insistent that the Christians in Philippi guard their minds by filtering their thoughts. If he were around today, he would challenge us with the same words.

With what do you fill your mind? Make sure it is true, noble, right, pure, lovely, admirable, excellent, and praiseworthy.

Finally, brothers, whatever is true, whatever is noble, whatever is right, whatever is pure, whatever is lovely, whatever is admirable—if anything is excellent or praiseworthy—think about such things.

PHILIPPIANS 4:8

PRAYER

Be aware of your thoughts today. Consider if they are pure, right, noble, and true—or if you would need less lovely adjectives to describe them! Ask the Lord to help you think purely.

You Are the Mighty King

And I praise Your name;
You are the Mighty King,
The Living Word,
Master of everything;
You are the Lord.

And I love Your name;
You are Almighty God,
Savior and Lord,
Wonderful Counselor;
You are the Lord.

And I love Your name;
You are the Prince of Peace,
Emmanuel, Everlasting Father;
You are the Lord.

—Eddie Espinosa

eter had his share of embarrassing moments. His tongue boasted footprints from the sandals that fit his feet. But one time Peter resisted the temptation to put his foot in his mouth.

Jesus asked the disciples what kind of press He was getting in the marketplace. "Who do people say the Son of Man is?" (Matthew 16:13). And His friends shared what they had heard as they had traveled around Israel. But then Jesus posed a follow-up question. "Who do you say I am?" And with enviable confidence Peter responded, "You are the Christ, the Son of the living God" (Matthew 16:15, 16).

If Jesus were to ask you the same set of questions, you probably could answer quite easily who people in your circle of influence think He is: either the Son of God or a respected religious prophet or teacher. Not much has changed in two thousand years. But how would you answer the second question? The temptation is to answer it the way Christians whom we admire would answer it. But Jesus would not be content with the stock answer. He wants to know who *you* say He is. If He isn't yet the Mighty King in your life, you can do something about that.

For to us a child is born, to us a son is given, and the government will be on his shoulders. And he will be called Wonderful Counselor, Mighty God, Everlasting Father, Prince of Peace.

ISAIAH 9:6

PRAYER

In the quiet of a reflective moment, listen for Jesus to ask you who He is in your life. Be honest. Then ask Him to become even more influential in your life.

J E S U S ,   W H A T   A   B E A U T I F U L   N A M E

Jesus—what a beautiful name!
Son of God, Son of Man,
Lamb that was slain.
Joy and peace, strength and hope.

Jesus—what a beautiful name!
Truth revealed, my future sealed,
Healed my pain.
Love and freedom, life and warmth.

Jesus—what a beautiful name!
Rescued my soul, my stronghold,
Lifts me from shame.
Forgiveness, security, power and love,
Grace that blows all fear away.

—TANYA RICHES

n angel caught a young teenage girl by surprise. The surprise element only grew when the angel proceeded to tell Mary what God had in mind. Before leaving her, the angel implied that a book of names would not be a necessary purchase. She was to call her baby "Jesus." But had Mary been told at that moment how the world would eventually be touched by the name of her Son, she would have been astounded.

In Mary's day, "Jesus" was a fairly common name. It was the Aramaic equivalent of Joshua. What was uncommon were the circumstances surrounding this particular Jesus' birth, His life and ministry, as well as His death and resurrection.

Today, baby boys are still named Jesus, especially in Latin American countries. But whenever you hear the name of Jesus without reference to a last name, there is no doubt about who is being talked about. He is the beautiful Savior with the beautiful name whose grace transforms the pain and sorrow of an ugly world and makes it a beautiful place to live.

"Jesus"—speak and sing that name with joy!

And his name will be the hope of all the world.

MATTHEW 12:21 (NLT)

PRAYER

Make the name of Jesus a work of art. Regardless of your artistic abilities, take crayons or markers and print JESUS in the middle of a blank sheet. Thank Him for the hope His name brings.

AS WE GATHER/
THE STEADFAST LOVE
OF THE LORD

As we gather, may Your Spirit work within us.
As we gather, may we glorify Your name,
Knowing well that as our hearts begin to
worship,
We'll be blessed because we came.

The steadfast love of the Lord never ceases;
His mercies never come to an end—
They are new every morning,
New every morning.
Great is Thy faithfulness, O Lord,
Great is Thy faithfulness.

—TOMMY COOMES AND MIKE FAY/EDITH MCNEILL

n the early 1970s something remarkable was happening in Costa Mesa, California. A pastor by the name of Chuck Smith walked the beaches of Orange County, sharing his faith in Jesus with long-haired hippies. As many gave their hearts to the Lord, Pastor Chuck suggested they gather for Bible study. Handfuls of converts became hundreds. Calvary Chapel became known as the church by the beach where lives were being changed nightly.

Pastor Chuck welcomed the new musical influences the converted hippies brought with them to Bible study and worship. He celebrated their gifts and invited them to write songs of praise to the Lord. The result was a movement in religious music that continues to this day.

The two songs that comprise this medley were part of the first wave of what we now refer to as praise and worship music. The evidence of changed lives, worship gatherings that were truly celebrations, and Spirit-inspired songs that reflected contemporary culture all bore witness to the steadfast love of the Lord that is continually new.

Regardless of your age, experience, or knowledge, you can sing your new song to the Lord.

It is of the LORD's mercies that we are not consumed, because his compassions fail not. They are new every morning: great is thy faithfulness.

LAMENTATIONS 3:22, 23 (KJV)

PRAYER

Thank God for the way praise music has touched your life and that of your family. Sing one of your favorite songs to the Lord—just you and Him.

D A Y   4 2

THE GREATEST THING

The greatest thing in all my life
Is knowing You.
The greatest thing in all my life
Is knowing You.
I want to know You more;
I want to know You more.
The greatest thing in all my life
Is knowing You.

—MARK PENDERGRASS

heaton College has had its share of notable graduates—including evangelist Billy Graham and martyred missionary Jim Elliott. These men left Wheaton with the school motto engraved on their hearts: "For Christ and His Kingdom."

In the days that followed September 11, 2001, the world was introduced to yet another graduate of Wheaton College. Todd Beamer, a 1991 graduate, was one of those on the United Airlines plane that crashed in rural Pennsylvania, a plane that was likely headed toward another target in Washington D.C. Todd and others on the plane with him are credited with leading an attack against the terrorists who had killed the pilot and commandeered the cockpit. Realizing he was about to die, Todd used the onflight phone to call home. Unable to reach his wife, he prayed the Lord's Prayer with the Air Fone operator as a testimony to his faith. Then he said good-bye and turned and uttered the phrase that has now been heard all over the world: "Let's roll!"

Knowing Christ and living for Him and His kingdom was Todd's highest priority. As a result, knowing that death was coming was not the end of the world. It didn't deter him from one final act of courageous Christian service. Living for Christ and His kingdom can motivate you to greatness too. Let's roll!

I want to know Christ and the power of his resurrection and the fellowship of sharing in his sufferings, becoming like him in his death.

PHILIPPIANS 3:10

PRAYER

Claim Wheaton College's motto as your prayer for today. Listen in your heart for ways the Lord will make aspects of that motto possible as you go about your tasks.

H I D E   M E   I N   Y O U R   H O L I N E S S

Hide me, Lord, in Your holiness;
Every sin I now confess.
Praise to You, forgiving Lord
Hide me in Your holiness.

Take my life, an offering—
All of me to You I bring.
Praise to You, O spotless Lamb!
Hide me in Your holiness.

Hide me, hide me, hide me, Lord.
Won't You hide me, hide me,
Hide me in Your holiness.
Hide me in Your holiness.

—STEVE RAGSDALE

o you recall the lullaby your mom used to sing to you as she rocked you to sleep? Probably not. And if your kids are pretty well grown, you might not even remember the lullabies you sang to them when they were babies. There are many from which to choose, but all nighty-night melodies have the same purpose—to provide an atmosphere of peace in which a little one can fall asleep.

When you think about it, this song resembles a lullaby. Its quiet soothing strains calm the spirit and comfort the soul. Even Steve Ragsdale's words have a lullaby quality to them. They definitely are the kind of thoughts you'd want to fill your mind at the end of the day.

After a grueling day of stressful decisions, anxious commutes, difficult encounters, and people issues, you want to relax in the presence of God. You want to confess your shortcomings and express your longings. As if with a blanket of protection, you desire for the Lord to hide you in His holy presence. Now there's a formula for a good night's sleep.

You are my hiding place; you will protect me from trouble and surround me with songs of deliverance.

PSALM 32:7

PRAYER

Tonight, surround yourself with this marvelous song. As you prepare to fall asleep, make the words of this comforting chorus your prayer.

THE SWEETEST
NAME OF ALL

Jesus, You're the sweetest name of all.

Jesus, You always hear me when I call.

Oh Jesus, You pick me up each time I fall;

You're the sweetest, the sweetest name of all.

—TOMMY COOMES

hen he was born, his mama named him Walter. But when Walter Payton grew up and started playing for the Chicago Bears, his fans called him "Sweetness." This Chicago Bear legend had the heart of a fierce competitor as well as the gentle heart of a compassionate person. On a team of tough football players, many of whom lacked some of the relational skills or social graces of other professions, Sweetness was a refreshing balance. When he died a few years ago in his early forties, Walter Payton had left the world a sweeter place.

No one in the Bible ever referred to Jesus as "Sweetness." Somehow that would have minimized the reverence of which He was worthy as the Messiah. But in a bitter world, where hate mocks love and justice is often pinned to the mat by power, Jesus came as the sweet foretaste of a glorious new world. Jesus was the sweet fragrance of life in a decaying world where death has taken a premature bow. His words of life were like honey.

No, Jesus was never called Sweetness, but His gentle, compassionate manner with children and society's outcasts was definitely more like sugar than vinegar. He desires to be the sweetener in your life as well. And He will be if you simply spend time in His presence each day.

How sweet are your words to my taste, sweeter than honey to my mouth.

PSALM 119:103 (NKJV)

PRAYER

Ask God to help you evaluate attitudes or patterns in your life that leave a sour taste in people's mouths. Seek His help to do just the opposite.

PEOPLE NEED THE LORD

Every day they pass me by;
I can see it in their eyes—
Empty people filled with care,
Headed who knows where.
On they go through private pain, living fear to fear.
Laughter hides their silent cries only Jesus hears.

We are called to take His light
To a world where wrong seems right.
What could be too great a cost
For sharing life with one who's lost?
Through His love our hearts can feel
All the grief they bear.
They must hear the words of life only we can share.

—GREG NELSON AND PHIL MCHUGH

ext time you are at the mall, conduct your own people survey. You'll need a clipboard, a sheet of paper, and a pencil. But don't worry. You won't need to ask questions. Just position yourself on a bench near to where shoppers walk as they trek from store to store. As people pass by, look in their faces. Write down descriptive words that describe what their faces convey. Do they look happy? Tired? Sorrowful? Pained? Bored? Energized? Depressed?

If they pass close enough to you, look into their eyes. What do you see? Light? Emptiness? Life? Passion? What about the body language you witness in the posture of individuals? Are they in love with life? Are they in a hurry? It's amazing what you can infer about people's level of contentment with life just by observing their countenance and actions.

If you could only peek into the souls of the people passing you, your heart would break. Yes, people need the Lord. You can see it in their eyes and on their faces. And because they need the Lord, they also need you to tell them about Him.

Who can you tell about the Savior today?

When he saw the crowds, he had compassion on them, because they were harassed and helpless, like sheep without a shepherd.

MATTHEW 9:36

PRAYER

Ask the Lord to give you eyes to see people in your world the way He does. Ask Him to break your heart with the things that break His heart.

L I F T   H I M   U P

I will come into Your presence, Lord,
With a sacrifice of praise,
With a song I will exalt You, Lord;
Blessed be Your holy name.

I will give You all the glory;
You delivered me from shame.
I'm created in Your righteousness;
Blessed be Your holy name.

Lift Him up; His name be lifted higher.
Lift Him up; exalt His holy name!
Lift Him up; His name be lifted higher;
Exalt His holy name!

—BILLY FUNK

f you have ever watched a weightlifting competition on television, you can describe the scene. A muscle-bound contestant resembling Hercules strides onto the stage wearing a body suit. As he prepares to reach down for the massive weights, his face takes on a certain aura. The lifter's eyes are closed. It's as if he is praying. Actually, he is lost in deep concentration. As he collects his thoughts, he is marshaling his strength for what is about to take place. And then after several moments of personal preparation, the athlete quickly jerks the bar up and pushes it over his head.

What a great parallel for the person who prepares to worship the Lord. In order to lift up the name of Jesus, we must thoughtfully prepare for what we are about to do. We need to focus our thoughts on the One we desire to worship. Closing our eyes to better concentrate, we may feel the need to confess wrong attitudes or sinful behavior. We no doubt will want to rehearse in our heads how the Lord has demonstrated His strength in the midst of our weakness. Much like the weightlifter who must mentally prepare himself for that which tests his limits, the awesome task of lifting the name of Jesus higher and higher requires us to go through a series of warm-up exercises.

I will praise you as long as I live, and in your name I will lift up my hands.

PSALM 63:4

PRAYER

Prepare to enter the Lord's holy presence by asking Him to reveal unconfessed sin in your life. Once He has, claim His offered forgiveness. Then spend some moments reflecting on His faithfulness.

H O S A N N A

Hosanna, hosanna in the highest!
Hosanna, hosanna in the highest!
Lord, we lift up Your name
With hearts full of praise;
Be exalted, oh Lord my God.
Hosanna in the highest!

Glory, glory to the King of kings!
Glory, glory to the King of kings!
Lord, we lift up Your name
With hearts full of praise;
Be exalted, oh Lord my God.
Glory to the King of kings!

—CARL TUTTLE

ids love parades. Something about a festive procession fuels their innate enthusiasm. The floats are beautiful. The bands are loud. The clowns are engaging. Have you ever seen an unhappy child while a parade passes by? Come to think of it, at parades adults most resemble their happy-go-lucky children. Smiles abound. Cares are absent.

Jerusalem's children lined the dusty road as a parade passed by one Sunday long ago. No clowns or bands. No flower-covered floats. No drill teams in this parade. But a dignitary was there. I guess you could say He was the Grand Marshal. The children cheered, but they were not alone. Their parents applauded and sang as the solitary figure riding a donkey came into view. "Hosanna! Hosanna in the highest!" they sang. They waved branches from palm trees. They carpeted the cobblestones with their capes and cloaks. The one on the donkey ironically was the King of the cosmos. It must have been quite a scene.

It's a scene that we are able to recreate every time we come as children into the Lord's presence. With joy and confidence we recognize there is no need to worry, for He is Lord of all.

The crowds that went ahead of him and those that followed shouted, "Hosanna to the Son of David! Blessed is he who comes in the name of the Lord! Hosanna in the highest!"

MATTHEW 21:9

PRAYER

Close your eyes and picture yourself at that Palm Sunday parade. Feel the enthusiastic joy. Think of words that you might have called out as you saw Jesus' smiling eyes looking in your direction.

THE RIVER IS HERE

Down the mountain the river flows,
And it brings refreshing wherever it goes,
Through the valleys and over the fields
The river is rushing, and the river is here.

The river of God sets our feet to dancing;
The river of God fills our hearts with cheer;
The river of God fills our mouths with
laughter,
And we rejoice for the river is here.

—ANDY PARK

I f you have ever had the privilege of traveling in Israel, you have probably visited Jerusalem, Bethlehem, and Nazareth. If you were fortunate, your tour also included the Jordan River which connects the Sea of Galilee and the Dead Sea. Consider yourself truly blessed if your itinerary encompassed Banias.

Banias (or ancient Dan) is the small territory to the north of Israel where the snowmelt of Mount Hermon cascades into flowing streams of fresh water before emptying into the Sea of Galilee. This lush green region feels like the Garden of Eden must have been. Unspoiled and fresh. Colorful and beautiful. As you walk the dirt paths at the base of the waterfalls, the churning sounds of the turbulent streams sound like a rhythmic melody.

What begins way up on the mountain as melting snow is in actuality the genesis of the Jordan River. What a great metaphor for the way the presence of a holy God flows into our lives. With small trickles of His grace and rivulets of His mercy, the river of God becomes a current that carries us with power each day of our lives. But we have a choice. We can dam the flow or let the Lord have His way. What will you choose today?

They are like trees planted along the riverbank, bearing fruit each season without fail. Their leaves never wither, and in all they do, they prosper.

PSALM 1:3 (NLT)

PRAYER

Thank God for the river of His love that flows continuously from His heart. Thank Him that it represents cleansing and healing.

D A Y   4 9

S H O U T   T O   T H E   N O R T H

Shout to the North and the South!
Sing to the East and the West.
Jesus is Savior to all—
Lord of Heaven and earth.

We've been through fire;
We've been through rain;
We've been refined by the power of His name.
We've fallen deeper in love with You;
You've burned the truth on our lips.

—M ARTIN S MITH

esus never claimed to be one of many ways to God. With an exclusive confidence that angers the contemporary critic of Christianity, jesus announced that He is "the way, the truth, and the life." Furthermore, without even pausing to take a breath, the Savior said, "No one can come to the Father except through me" (John 14:6, NLT).

Someone has joked that to say that "all religions lead to God" is like saying that to call home all you need to do is simply dial any seven digits you choose. All calls end up at the same place. Only a fool would try that approach. Obviously, every set of numbers but one would be wrong.

The truth is, Jesus is the Savior for all. He did not die for only a certain type of person. He died for the world He created. He seeks a relationship with people of every color, every language group, and every culture in every country of the world. What might initially sound exclusive or narrow is, in fact, grounded in glorious inclusivity. We are invited to call out to the ends of the earth that God so loved the world that He gave His only Son that whoever believes in Him will not perish but have everlasting life.

Messenger of good news, shout to Zion from the mountaintops! Shout louder to Jerusalem—do not be afraid. Tell the towns of Judah, "Your God is coming!"

ISAIAH 40:9 (NLT)

PRAYER

The "shout" is a biblical form of praise. Why not try it? In your prayer closet, the basement or alone in the woods, go ahead and cheer the Lord with a "hallelujah" or an "I praise you, Jesus!"

YOU ARE GOD

You.

You are.

You are God.

You are God, God, God.

You are God
In what seems like happenstance.
You are God in ev'ry circumstance.
You are God when we fall
And God when we stand;
You are God who holds us
In Your hand.

—SCOTT UNDERWOOD

e are imperfect people who have a tendency to be capricious, moody, and unreliable. We say one thing and do another. We make promises only to let those easily spoken words fall from our lips and break in a million pieces on the ground. We were created in God's image, but we are damaged goods. Sometimes we resemble our Creator; sometimes we fail the likeness test miserably.

In contrast to our unpredictability, God is constant, true, and faithful. He can only be consistent with Himself. The Scriptures tell us that He is incapable of change. What He promises, He does. What He prizes, He continues to treasure. What He demands, He continues to expect. Although some would argue to the contrary, His Ten Commandments have not become ten suggestions. His fallen world is still a world for which He continues to accept responsibility and is one over which He maintains complete control.

Simply said, our changing views about God don't alter God. Our inability to accept His truth does not invalidate its accuracy. God is God and will always be. This is a terribly frightening and yet a very comforting reality. It is a reality that invites our praise.

Every good and perfect gift is from above, coming down from the Father of the heavenly lights, who does not change like shifting shadows.

JAMES 1:17

PRAYER

Admit to God your tendency to be hot or cold (even lukewarm) toward Him. Ask Him to increase your faithfulness. Celebrate the fact that He cannot change.

YOU ARE MY KING

I'm forgiven because You were forsaken.
I'm accepted; You were condemned.
I'm alive and well; Your Spirit is within me
Because You died and rose again.

Amazing love! How can it be
That You, my King, would die for me?
Amazing love! I know it's true;
It's my joy to honor You.

In all I do I honor you;
You are my King, You are my King.
Jesus, You are my King; Jesus, You are my King.

—BILLY JAMES FOOTE

here's no such thing as a free lunch. That old axiom means that there has to be somebody footing the bill somewhere. Those who make their way to a soup kitchen or a rescue mission don't have to pay at the door. They are welcome. But someone has contributed to this agency so it could provide for others.

The same could be said for heaven's handout. Looking down on His fallen creation, God saw us in our need. We could not repair the rift that separated us from our Creator. Heaven was designed to be our ultimate home, but without some kind of intervention we would be forever homeless. A holy God who is wholly compassionate designed a rescue mission that would bridge the breach. He would offer us complete forgiveness, residency in heaven, and full inheritance as sons and daughters. But the only way He could accomplish this was to punish His perfect Son by placing on Him all our guilt, shame, and selfish ambition. Grace would be free, but it would come with an unbelievably costly price tag.

No wonder we call it "amazing" grace. In light of all Jesus did to purchase our salvation, no wonder we claim Him as the King of our lives.

For you know the grace of our Lord Jesus Christ, that though he was rich, yet for your sakes he became poor, so that you through his poverty might become rich.

2 CORINTHIANS 8:9

PRAYER

Consider the contrasts that distinguish us from our great God. Think about what the Father paid that we might freely claim His love.

ONCE AGAIN

Jesus Christ, I think upon Your sacrifice:
You became nothing poured out to death.
Many times I've wondered at Your gift of life,
And I'm in that place once again;
And I'm in that place once again.

Once again I look upon the cross where You died;
I'm humbled by Your mercy, and I'm broken inside.
Once again I thank You;
Once again I pour out my life.

Thank You for the cross,
Thank You for the cross,
Thank You for the cross.

—MATT REDMAN

he kitchen table represents the heart of a family unit. Around it, a memorized grace is offered, meals are shared, and memories are made. Parents rebuke, siblings tease, heartaches are confessed, and jokes are tried on for size. To this same table, grown children who had married and scattered return, time and time again to see the folks and recall the good old days. When a family member dies, the kitchen table serves as a magnet, drawing the mourning to assigned places.

In much the same way, the communion table at church serves as the family gathering place. As we gather around this family table, memories are recalled that point to the death of our elder Brother who willed that we would forever gather in His name. Like the one in the home in which we grew up, this is also a table where we can expect the Father's discipline, assurance of His forgiveness, and the opportunity to celebrate the privilege of being a family.

Whenever you have an occasion to enjoy the Lord's Supper, once again you are given an opportunity to think about Jesus' sacrifice and embrace the inheritance of His grace. Thank Him for the cross, for by it you have been saved.

He canceled the record that contained the charges against us. He took it and destroyed it by nailing it to Christ's cross.

COLOSSIANS 2:14 (NLT)

PRAYER

Use a cross pendant or a cross on the wall as a visual aid. Think about the cross on which the Savior paid for your salvation. Ponder His suffering. Meditate on His love.

P O U R   O U T   M Y   H E A R T

Here I am once again—
I pour out my heart for I know that You hear
Every cry; You are listening,
No matter what state my heart is in.

Pour out my heart to say that I love You;
Pour out my heart to say that I need You;
Pour out my heart to say that I'm thankful;
Pour out my heart to say that You're wonderful.

—CRAIG MUSSEAU

f you knew for a fact that God heard you every time you prayed, you'd be inclined to keep praying, right? If you were convinced that God caringly bent His ear in your direction whenever you approached Him with something that was on your heart, you'd be more apt to come clean with Him. So why do we typically struggle to maintain a regular prayer time?

Maybe it's related to questions we have about how prayer works. If God is really interested in what we have to say and if He actually listens to the cry of our heart, does He actually answer the prayers we offer up?

Scripture is definitive about this. It assures us that God answers every prayer we pray—every single one. His answers aren't always the ones we're expecting or hoping for. But He always responds. Sometimes God replies with yes, sometimes with no, sometimes with wait.

So don't look at prayer as an obligation that you need to do to please God. Accept it as a wonderful privilege to pour out your heart to Someone who cares for you more than anyone else in the world.

Trust in him at all times, O people; pour out your hearts to him, for God is our refuge.

PSALM 62:8

PRAYER

It's called "emptying prayer." Take out a blank sheet of paper and write as fast as you can all the "stuff" in your heart about which you are concerned. Transfer the title of these worries to the Lord.

B L E S S   T H E   L O R D ,
O   M Y   S O U L

Bless the Lord, oh my soul
And all that is within me;
Bless His holy name.

He has done great things;
He has done great things;
He has done great things;
Bless His holy name.

—PETE SANCHEZ, JR.

t's the funniest thing. You are stopped at a red light when look over to your right, and there in the car next to you is a nattily dressed businessman engaged in an animated conversation . . . with himself—a classic case of insanity. The driver smiles, punctuating his thoughts with hand gestures. One moment he is losing it with laughter. And then before the light has changed to green, he is chewing himself out royally. Oh, now you see it. He isn't talking to himself after all. His car is equipped with a wireless phone attached to the sun visor.

Quite possibly, those who observed King David on his throne thought he was off his rocker. He did not have a miniature cell phone clipped to his royal robes, yet he was talking to himself. The Scriptures bear witness to that. And based on what the Word of God indicates, nothing about David's practice betrayed mental illness. He spoke to his soul.

Come to think of it, following David's practice might very well *prevent* mental illness or emotional captivity. When we command our inner beings to rejoice in the Lord, we place ourselves in position to do more than just respond to negative feelings or unexpected circumstances. By talking to ourselves, we discover the benefits of being proactive.

Bless the LORD, O my soul; and all that is within me, bless His holy name!

PSALM 103:1 (NKJV)

PRAYER

Instead of reeling off requests of what you want God to do for you, picture yourself in the presence of the Lord, all the while speaking aloud to your soul. Remind yourself how wonderful He is.

I   S I N G   P R A I S E S

I sing praises to Your name, oh Lord,

Praises to Your name, oh Lord,

For Your name is great

And greatly to be praised.

I give glory to Your name, oh Lord,

Glory to Your name, oh Lord,

For Your name is great

And greatly to be praised.

—TERRY MACALMON

obert Schmidgall was the beloved pastor of the 4,000-member Calvary Church in Naperville, Illinois. He and his wife, Karen, had planted the church in their living room thirty years earlier. Through their influence, hundreds of people had put their trust in Christ and discovered the indescribable joy of worshiping Him. Bob Schmidgall loved to sing praises, and he continued to lead the congregation in singing praise.

On January 3, 1998, two days after he had celebrated his 55th birthday, Pastor Bob collapsed while having breakfast with a friend in a local restaurant. He was dead by the time he hit the floor.

On the day of his funeral, the sanctuary of Calvary Church was packed to capacity. Seated among members of the congregation were the mayor, city council members, and ministerial colleagues. It should have surprised no one that, as Pastor Bob's casket was rolled up the center aisle and positioned near the communion table at the front of the church, the congregation was led in singing this song, "I Sing Praises." Because that was this pastor's stated goal in life, it was only appropriate that these lyrics would mark his death.

What song would epitomize your life and Christian commitment?

Praise the LORD. Sing to the LORD a new song, his praise in the assembly of the saints.

PSALM 149:1

PRAYER

Thank the Lord for those pastors, Sunday school teachers, and church leaders whom He has used in your life to sow and nurture faith. Ask the Lord to use you in the lives of others.

THE POTTER'S HAND

Beautiful Lord, wonderful Savior,

I know for sure all of my days

Are held in Your hand and crafted into Your perfect

plan.

You gently call me into Your presence,

Guiding me by Your Holy Spirit.

Teach me, dear Lord,

To live all of my life through Your eyes.

I'm captured by Your holy calling; set me apart.

I know You're drawing me to Yourself.

Lead me, Lord, I pray;

Take me, mold me, use me, fill me;

I give my life to the Potter's hand.

Call me, guide me, lead me, walk beside me;

I give my life to the Potter's hand.

—DARLENE ZSCHECH

he story is told of a master pottery maker in Peru. Having heard of the distinct quality of his work, people from all over the world traveled to the outskirts of Lima in search of his unpretentious shop. It was an uncovered, cluttered workspace exposed to the intense rays of the South American sun. As a result of forty years of continuous labor, the potter's sun-baked skin resembled the dark reddish-brown clay he shaped into beautiful pots and bowls.

What distinguished this artisan's pottery was a small indentation that every piece boasted. The notchlike feature at first glance might be considered a flaw. But it was not. It was the result of a clawlike digit on the potter's right hand. He was born with it instead of thumb. The shriveled stub and its permanent sharp fingernail imprinted the clay as it was fashioned in its final form. What had been a source of endless humiliation as a child had become the signature of success.

Although our Creator's fashioning hands are not deformed, as He shapes us into His image, the evidence of His fingerprints in our lives render us valuable and priceless in His eyes. Celebrate the worth He sees as He looks at you today.

Yet, O LORD, you are our Father. We are the clay, you are the potter; we are all the work of your hand.

ISAIAH 64:8

PRAYER

Hold out your hands in front you. Observe the tiny blotches, the wrinkles, the unique markings of your palm. Allow the mystery of your hands to remind you of the loving purpose with which the Potter shaped your life.

L I F T   H I G H   T H E
L O R D ,   O U R   B A N N E R

Lift high the Lord, our banner.
Lift high the Lord Jesus, King.
Lift high the Lord, our banner.
Lift high your praise to Him, sing.

For He is wonderful!
For He reigns on high!
For He is marvelous!
The Lord draweth nigh.

—MACON DELAVAN

ver since Sept 11th, there has been a renewed interest in flying Old Glory. Miniature flags flutter from antennas as cars fly down the freeway. Giant flags hang majestic and motionless in food courts of shopping malls. Residential neighborhoods are punctuated by the prominence of stars and stripes positioned on front porches.

When our freedoms are threatened, our fearful hearts beat as one. We are willing to proudly gather under the banner of our country without concern of being criticized. When war looms, there is no room for cynics.

Obviously, Old Glory has its place. But we who are citizens of another kingdom know that the Lord is our glory. He is our banner. He is the emblem of our salvation. He is our standard of righteousness. Because the cross has staked His claim in the soil of our souls, it is only right that we pledge to Him our allegiance.

Songs that remind us that we are subjects of the King do not undermine the love of our country. They provide us with a necessary reality check that when all is said and done, our kingdom has yet to fully come.

But we are citizens of heaven, where the Lord Jesus Christ lives. And we are eagerly waiting for him to return as our Savior.

PHILIPPIANS 3:20 (NLT)

PRAYER

Thank God for the blessings and privilege of living in a country that allows you the freedom of worship. But don't stop there. Ask the Lord to put in your heart a longing for heaven.

MIGHTY WARRIOR

Mighty warrior dressed for battle,
Holy Lord of all is He.
Commander in chief, bring us to attention;
Lead us into battle to crush the enemy.

Satan has no authority here in this place;
He has no authority here,
For this habitation was fashioned for the
Lord's presence.
No authority here.

Jesus has all authority here in this place;
He has all authority here,
For this habitation was fashioned for the
Lord's presence.
All authority here!

—DEBBYE GRAAFSMA

hen you think of commanders in chief, who comes to mind? Ulysses S. Grant? Robert E. Lee? George Patton? Dwight D. Eisenhower? In the United States, the term refers to the president. He is the head of all those in the armed services. He is the apex of the military chain of command. No wonder a trumpet fanfare hails his entrance whenever he enters a room. He is vested with total authority and willingly bears the responsibility for the nation's defense.

Referring to Jesus as the Commander in Chief of the cosmic battle of the ages is appropriate. It's a great word picture. Christ went head to head against the guerilla-like strategies of Satan and won. Thinking of Him as the Mighty Warrior, who stands with us as we face our daily spiritual skirmishes, is a wonderful word picture. Although we may feel as though we are all alone on the front lines, nothing could be further from the truth. Our Warrior is with us, leading us through the trenches and providing us with a barrage of protection. Going before us, His shadow falls upon us and envelops us with safety.

Then Jesus came to them and said, "All authority in heaven and on earth has been given to me."
MATTHEW 28:18

PRAYER

Admit your feelings of weakness and vulnerability to Jesus. Confess your need of His protection and strength. Picture Him helping you put on your spiritual armor.

HOW GREAT IS YOUR LOVE

No eye has seen, and no ear has heard,
And no mind has ever conceived
The glorious things
That You have prepared for ev'ryone who has
believed.
You brought us near, and You called us Your own
And made us joint heirs with Your Son.

How high and how wide,
How deep and how long,
How sweet and how strong is Your love!
How lavish Your grace,
How faithful Your ways,
How great is Your love, oh Lord!

—MARK ALTROGGE

ow deep is your love?" Long before the Bee Gees posed that question as a way of measuring romantic affection, the apostle Paul considered it in terms of God's love. Digging to the point of bedrock, Paul strained with everything he had to try and picture for us the dimensions of our spiritual security. The pile of words that resulted from his dredging expedition fills the eighth chapter of Romans.

Suffice it to say, there is no way that we can comprehend the greatness of God's love. It goes beyond our ability to understand or communicate (let alone measure). To say it is higher than a mountain and wider than the heavens is only the beginning. The love of God is the source of our faith, the destination of our hope, and the means by which we can love Him in return. Far more than some adolescent definition of infatuation, God's love is the unfathomable, indescribable atmosphere that allows us to breathe spiritually. In His unconditional love, acceptance, and forgiveness is the oxygen of life. Consciously breathe in His love as you go about your day.

For I am convinced that neither death nor life, neither angels nor demons, neither the present nor the future, nor any powers, neither height nor depth, nor anything else in all creation, will be able to separate us from the love of God that is in Christ Jesus our Lord.

ROMANS 8:38, 39

PRAYER

Thank the Lord for His love that is so high, wide, deep, and long that it always surrounds you.

I L I F T M Y E Y E S U P
(P S A L M 1 2 1)

I lift my eyes up to the mountains,
Where does my help come from?
My help comes from You—
Maker of heaven, Creator of the earth.

Oh how I need You, Lord;
You are my only hope.
So I will wait for You to come and rescue me,
Come and give me life.

—BRIAN DOERKSEN

he ancient city of Jerusalem was not all that big. "The Ophel,"
as the city of David was called, was about a mile long and a
half-mile wide. This rectangular-shaped strip of land gently sloped
north across the Kidron Valley from the Mount of Olives. In this same
section of land Solomon would later build the temple of the Lord.

Because of the topography of the area, the location of Israel's
capital city was always a concern. It was precariously perched among
the Judean hills. Because taller hills encircled the city, Jerusalem was
vulnerable to sneak attacks by her enemies.

The King James Version of Psalm 121 is beautiful poetry, but it
offers a misleading translation. "I will lift up mine eyes unto the hills,
from whence cometh my help" gives the impression that the hills were
a symbolic source of strength. They were not at all. They were a source
of fear. Fortunately, newer translations remedy the situation. Because
the king lifts his eyes up to the mountains, naturally he wonders where
his help will come from. And, gratefully, he can answer for us based on
his past experiences. His help will come from the Lord who made
heaven and earth. When you need help, you need only to lift your eyes
to heaven. From there, your help will come.

*I lift up my eyes to the hills—where does my help come from? My help comes from the
Lord, the Maker of heaven and earth.*

PSALM 121:1, 2

PRAYER

By what mountains do you feel dwarfed today? What issues leave you feel intimidated or afraid? Lay
them before the Lord and express gratitude that God promises His help.

E X A L T   T H E   L O R D

Exalt the Lord our God!
Exalt the Lord our God
And worship at His holy hill,
For the Lord our God,
His name is holy.

We worship You, Lord, for Your name is holy,
We worship You, Lord, for Your name is holy.

—RICK RIDINGS

ave you ever been caught in the middle of an unexpected rain shower on a warm spring day? Because the weather forecaster didn't anticipate this sudden change in barometric pressure, he or she failed to advise you of the need for an umbrella. As a result, you got absolutely drenched. But you didn't mind all that much. It was a warm rain and actually heaven's "tears of joy" felt kind of nice.

It's a bit odd. Being caught unawares and getting soaked do not exactly define an ideal situation. But if the above scenario has ever been your plight, you know how delightful it is. You wouldn't want it any other way.

Something just as unexpected and wonderful is the refreshing presence of the unseen Lord. You can't see Him, but you feel Him near. This beautiful praise song is a mellow reminder of how perfect our lives can seem even when they are lived against the backdrop of big disappointments. Go ahead and play this song once again and let the showers of God's love drench your heart with the reminder that He is in control. We exalt Him when we relax in the knowledge of His sovereignty.

I will cause my people and their homes around my holy hill to be a blessing. And I will send showers, showers of blessings, which will come just when they are needed.

Ezekiel 34:26 (nlt)

PRAYER

Stop right now. Don't go any further. Your plans for the day will wait. Spend the next five minutes realigning your perspective. Claim the promise that the Lord is with you in all that you do.

G R E A T   A R E   Y O U   L O R D /
G R E A T   I S   T H Y   N A M E

Great are You, Lord, worthy of praise,

Holy and true. Great are You, Lord,

Most holy Lord.

O precious Lord, great is Thy name;

Great is Thy name, O precious Lord.

Great is Thy name in all the earth.

Great is Thy name,

Great is Thy name,

Great is Thy name in all the earth.

—STEVE COOK AND VIKKI COOK/DAN MARKS

ack in the sixties, Tony the Tiger loved to growl out his reaction to his special cereal: "They're gr-r-r-eat!" he'd say. It was an advertiser's clever attempt to get us kids to bug our parents to buy that brand. Well, even though it's probably been quite a while since you last had a bowl for breakfast, you have to admit they were good. Maybe even very good. But *great?*

Life is filled with all kinds of special things—favorite foods, heartrending music, breathtaking beauty, poignant moments with family, career milestones, birth, maturity, reconciliation and so much more. As incredibly moving as these experiences are, however, we do ourselves a disservice if we are quick to claim that they are *great*. Only God is great. Only He is deserving of such a five-star rating. Only He is perfect. Consider this acronym: "God Rules Everything Always Terrifically." Now that's gr-r-r-eat!

As with the word "love," when we overuse a word that (by definition) is to be used sparingly, it loses its punch. Next time you catch yourself saying something is really great, rewind the tape and replace the adjective. Meanwhile, take time today to be conscious of all that is great about our great God.

Great is the LORD and most worthy of praise; his greatness no one can fathom.

PSALM 145:3

PRAYER

Come up with your own acronym for God's greatness using the five letters of the word "g-r-e-a-t." Meditate prayerfully on your great God.

I W I L L S E R V E T H E E

I will serve You because I love You;
You have given life to me.
I was nothing until You found me;
You have given life to me.

Heartaches, broken people,
Ruined lives are why You died on Calvary.
Your touch is what I long for;
You have given life to me.

—GLORIA GAITHER AND WILLIAM J. GAITHER

n the film version of *Annie*, that little red-haired orphan girl is chauffeured to Daddy Warbucks's mansion. Mr. Warbucks's assistant describes to Annie all the wonderful opportunities that await her. She will be able to have tennis lessons, go swimming, shop for new clothes, and choose what she would like for dinner. The list goes on and on.

Because Annie is accustomed to earning her keep at the orphanage, when she is asked what she would like to do first, the little orphan girl stops to think, then says, "I think I'll do the windows first and then the floors, so in case I spill water on the floor I can mop it up while scrubbing." When told she doesn't have to do any chores in her new home, Annie can't believe it. It sounds too good to be true.

Being adopted into the family of God is a lot like Annie's experience. Becoming heirs of God is nothing we can earn. It's a free gift. Salvation and eternal life are bequeathed to us. All the same, recognizing what has been given to us (and can't be taken away), we are overwhelmed with love and want to serve the Lord as a way of saying thanks. What we do is a way of expressing our love.

But be sure to fear the LORD and serve him faithfully with all your heart; consider what great things he has done for you.

1 SAMUEL 12:24

PRAYER

Before you ask God to do something for you today, make yourself available to Him and listen for ways that He might want you to serve Him.

U N T O   T H E   K I N G

Now unto the King eternal,
Unto the King immortal,
Unto the King invisible,
The only wise God,
The only wise God.

Unto the King be glory and honor,
Unto the King forever.
Unto the King be glory and honor,
Forever and ever amen.

—JOEY HOLDER

egend records that when she was a little girl, Queen Elizabeth got separated from her parents while on a hike in a forest. Afraid and alone, the young princess followed a path until she came to a cottage. An elderly woman welcomed the child into her home and proceeded to brew a pot of tea. Elizabeth explained her plight and asked for help. The woman, in whose home the princess sought refuge, was most impressed with Elizabeth's etiquette and grace. Eventually she asked the child, "Are you someone special?" to which Elizabeth answered, "Oh no, mum. I'm no one particularly special. But my father is the king!"

What a wonderful picture of who we are and what we are called to be! In the grand scheme of things, we aren't all that insignificant. We are easily lost in the jungle of life. We are in need of others to help us find direction. But our Father is the King of the universe. He has everything under control and is not overcome by the challenges that steal our peace. As we focus our eyes on Him instead of the obstacles around us, not only will we discover an ability to cope, we will reflect His grace and beauty. As we look to Him today, those around us will see in us a family resemblance.

Now unto the King eternal, immortal, invisible, the only wise God, be honour and glory for ever and ever. Amen.

I TIMOTHY 1:17 (KJV)

PRAYER

Celebrate the freedom you have being a creature and not the Creator. Thank God that you are not responsible for the holding the world together. Express gratitude that He is.

THE LORD IS HOLY

The Lord is holy, the Lord is holy;
We give Him glory and honor and praise.
The Lord is holy, the Lord is holy,
Holy and just righteous in all His ways.

Blessed is he who comes in the name of the Lord.
Blessed is he and worthy of praises outpoured.
Heaven and earth are full of His glory and grace;
It's the Lord who comes to inhabit this place.

—WALT HARRAH

preschool boy rushed into the kitchen while his mother was preparing dinner. Having played outside in a vacant lot since lunch, the little guy was covered with dirt, grass stains, and thistles. A forest of muddy footprints followed behind him as he hurried into the house. Before his mom could utter a word, Josh held up both arms and said, "I need a bath, Mommy. I'm a filthy, dirty mess. Can you help me get clean?"

The consequence of living in a fallen world includes falling down and getting smudged with the filth that surrounds us. We are stained by the ugly talk we hear at work. The atmosphere of gossip, off-colored stories, and profanity rubs off on us. We get tripped up by jealousy, envy, and a desire to please other people. We get snagged by temptations that arouse our lower nature. Yes, we know what it feels like to need a bath. We are anything but holy.

Gratefully, the God we worship is holy and pure. He longs to cleanse us from the evidence of sin in our lives and in our world. Memories of that warm, soapy washcloth with which our moms used to bathe us whet our desire to be clean before the Lord.

Cleanse me with hyssop, and I will be clean; wash me, and I will be whiter than snow.

PSALM 51:7

PRAYER

On a sheet of paper, jot down thoughts or actions that marked your life in a negative way today. Admit your weakness and wrongdoing to the Lord. Accept His cleansing.

DAY 66

HIS NAME IS JESUS

His name is Jesus, Jesus;
Sad hearts weep no more.
He has healed the brokenhearted,
Opened wide the prison doors;
He is able to deliver evermore.

—G. M. BILLS

hristians have been singing songs of praise since the first century. One of the very first songs they sang is actually recorded in correspondence Paul wrote to the church in Philippi. In the second chapter of Philippians, he incorporates lyrics into his letter about the incarnation of God's Son. Those ancient words underscore the uniqueness of Jesus. They celebrate the fact that His name is above every other name.

The life and ministry of Jesus bore witness to the truth that nothing could derail the locomotive power of His love. The lame walked, the blind saw, the dead were raised to life. When Jesus encountered need, He sowed seeds of hope. And the reason was clear—He had the upper hand.

Throughout history, those who claim the name of Jesus watch walls of resistance fall. The name of Jesus continues to take precedence over every other name that defines humanity today: Sinner, Blindness, Prisoner, and Orphan. It is a name that is elevated above Death, Demon Possession, Drug Addiction, or Divorce. It is a name that we are given permission to speak when confronted with the giants that dwarf us each day. All we need to do is speak it boldly and watch the Lord intervene on our behalf.

Therefore God exalted him to the highest place and gave him the name that is above every name, that at the name of Jesus every knee should bow.

PHILIPPIANS 2:9, 10

PRAYER

Softly say the name of Jesus over and over again. Each time you say it, picture it rising to the top of the pyramid of pain and problems in your life. Thank him that he is "king of your mountain."

ALL-CONSUMING FIRE

All-consuming fire, You're my heart's desire,
And I love You dearly, dearly Lord.
You're my meditation and my consolation,
And I love You dearly, dearly Lord.

Glory to the Lamb!
I exalt the great I AM!
Reigning on Your glorious throne,
You are my eternal home.

—RANDY N. WRIGHT

ollowing the collapse of the two towers of the World Trade Center, the smoldering rubble burned for months. As bodies were retrieved and debris carried away, smoke continued to curl toward the sky, reminding us of a tragedy we'd rather forget. Gratefully, the burning eventually ceased as peace returned to our hearts.

Scripture tells us that our God is an all-consuming fire. Unlike the hell on earth that follows the invasion of an enemy, His is not a fire that blazes without purpose. His eternal flame is a purifying fire. It is fueled by His holiness. It is spread by His desire that we be holy, too. His smokeless flame aims to burn away our impure motives and consume our wayward thoughts. With the heat of a refiner's furnace, the Lord desires to rid us of anything that would stand between Him and us.

Although the ravaging smoke of September 11th speaks of the sin in our world that God wills to quench, the blazing fire of an Olympic torch or the flickering flame of a dinner-table candle can be a helpful reminder of the presence of a holy God. He is the God of every nation and a God who focuses His cleansing love in our direction.

Therefore, since we are receiving a kingdom that cannot be shaken, let us be thankful, and so worship God acceptably with reverence and awe, for our God is a consuming fire.

HEBREWS 12:28, 29

PRAYER

Light a candle and ponder the dancing flame. Read the verse from Hebrews and ask the Lord what impurity in your life He desires to burn away today.

ALL THINGS ARE POSSIBLE

Almighty God, my Redeemer,
My hiding place, my safe refuge,
No other name like Jesus;
No power can stand against You.

My feet are planted on this rock,
And I will not be shaken.
My hope it comes from You alone,
My Lord and my salvation.

When I am weak, You make me strong;
When I'm poor, I know I'm rich,
For in the power of Your name
All things are possible.

—DARLENE ZSCHECH

inda Gregoriev thought her life was over. Her husband, Steve, had just died leaving her with five adopted children under the age of twelve. This forty-something schoolteacher doubted she would ever marry again. "Who would want a widow with five kids?" she wondered. As far as she was concerned, it would more likely that she be kidnapped by a Middle Eastern sheik than find a husband.

But Linda had not given her Savior the credit He deserved. As a committed Christian, she knew that Jesus delights in drilling doors through steel curtains. But a lack of faith prevented her from believing the Lord for such a miracle in her situation. Nonetheless, the Lord was determined to surprise Linda with proof that He is the God of the impossible.

Enter a recently converted recovering alcoholic by the name of Larry. Making himself available to do "fix-up" projects around Linda's home, Larry found himself falling in love. The widow's contagious smile and compassionate heart won his. Not only were the two married, within two years they were accepted by Wycliffe Bible Translators as field staff in South America. All things possible? You'd better believe it.

Jesus looked at them and said, "With man this is impossible, but with God all things are possible."
MATTHEW 19:26

PRAYER

Think about some situation in your life or that of an acquaintance where the Lord lived up to His reputation as the God of the impossible. Then praise Him!

B L E S S E D   B E   T H E   L O R D

Blessed be the Lord, a mighty fortress;
Blessed be the Lord, my sword and shield;
Blessed be the Lord who reigns victorious;
Blessed be the name of the Lord.
Your power is like the raging sea;
Your grace brought it down to me.
And now I walk in victory;
Blessed be the name of the Lord.

Your blood set this captive free,
Your love is giving life to me,
And now I'm Yours eternally;
Blessed be the name of the Lord.

—JEFF HAMLIN

arly in the 16th century, only those schooled in Latin could read the Scriptures. That basically meant the leaders of the Catholic Church. Martin Luther thought something should be done about that. It seemed discriminatory. But because of his determination to change the situation, he found himself imprisoned in a German castle. His heinous crime? Translating the Bible into the language of his countrymen. As he contemplated his fate, he was able to contrast his impenetrable confines to the fortresslike protection that God offers to every Christian.

Luther picked up his quill and, dipping it in a bottle of black ink, scrawled lyrics about the security of the believer that could be sung to a popular drinking tune. Yes, nearly five hundred years later Christians are still singing, "A Mighty Fortress Is Our God."

Martin Luther was right. We are secure in the protection of a loving God. Even when we are misunderstood or falsely accused, we are not defenseless. We may feel vulnerable to attack or weak as can be, but God is an ever-present help in time of need.

God is our refuge and strength, an ever-present help in trouble. Therefore we will not fear, though the earth give way and the mountains fall into the heart of the sea.

PSALM 46:1, 2

PRAYER

What has you locked in a prison tower? Some unsubstantiated fear? Let the Lord remind you that He is your tower of strength. Ask Him for the faith to trust Him.

WE BELIEVE

We believe in God the Father,
Maker of the universe,
And in Christ, His Son, our Savior,
Come to us by virgin birth.
We believe He died to save us,
Bore our sins, was crucified;
Then from death He rose victorious,
Ascended to the Father's side.
Jesus, Lord of all, Lord of all.

—GRAHAM KENDRICK

hat do we believe? This song, taken from the ancient Apostles' Creed, condenses the Christian faith into a few lines that describe what believers across the world believe. While we may have different opinions about many things, we are in complete agreement about these: We believe in God the Father, the Creator, and in Christ, His Son, who was born of a virgin, suffered to save us, and then rose again. We look forward to life everlasting.

The God to whom we cling by faith is the one who made all there is. And though He calls each star by name, He also calls us His own children. In His eternal heart of love, He conceived of a way to embrace a sinful world. We believe this Way to be the Truth and the Life.

We believe He's the Savior of all. Jesus became the innocent victim of suffering as He died for us. But He pried himself free from Death's icy fingers and flew to the realm of heaven beyond to a seat of high honor, reserved only for Him since before even time began.

Our beliefs aren't owned only by us. We share them with millions who commune with us from Christ's cup, all the while looking up with grateful hearts, thankful for our forgiveness and for the life yet to come.

We believe that Jesus died and rose again and so we believe that God will bring with Jesus those who have fallen asleep in him.

1 THESSALONIANS 4:14

PRAYER

Contemplate Jesus Christ, the risen and glorified Lord, seated on His throne. Come boldly into His presence convinced that He died to make your relationship with Him possible.

BEHOLD WHAT MANNER OF LOVE

Behold what manner of love
The Father has given unto us.
Behold what manner of love
The Father has given unto us,
That we should be called
The sons of God,
That we should be called
The sons of God.

—PATRICIA VAN TINE

ugh Everett struggled with self-esteem. Six months after he was born, his unwed mother determined she could not raise him and deposited him at an orphanage. For the next two years, little Hugh was farmed out to foster home after foster home. Each time he was returned and branded unadoptable. At last a couple unable to conceive took Hugh home. Shortly thereafter they succeeded in having a child of their own. Favoring their natural-born son, the couple often ignored Hugh. He grew up aching to know the love of birth parents he would never meet.

Although the family in which he was raised was not religious, a requirement of his adoption was that he be provided religious instruction. So each week the couple would drop Hugh off at Ruth Morton Baptist Church down the street from their home. At this small church, young Hugh heard about a heavenly Father with whom a relationship of love is possible. Hugh responded with eagerness, and the ache in his heart desiring to belong was at long-last filled.

Today Hugh Everett is an esteemed author of thirty biographies. In each book he celebrates the story of God's faithfulness in the life of his subject and also celebrates his own sense of identity.

Behold, what manner of love the Father hath bestowed upon us, that we should be called the sons of God: therefore the world knoweth us not, because it knew him not.

1 JOHN 3:1 (KJV)

PRAYER

Thank God for the parents He gave you (even if they were less than ideal). Now, contemplate the perfection of parental love that your heavenly Father channels in your direction.

STAND IN THE CONGREGATION

I will stand in the congregation,
And I will exalt You.
I will stand in the congregation,
And I will exalt You.
Let the children of Your salvation
Lift their praises too:
Hallelujah, hallelujah!

Hallelujah, hallelujah,
Hallelujah, hallelujah!
You're the only inspiration
For my praise, O God.

—BILL BATSTONE

ack in the 1960s, the Mexico branch of Wycliffe Bible Translators was housed in Mexico City in an old hotel called The Kettle. Wycliffe's founder, William Cameron Townsend, would often lead Sunday night gatherings. There was enthusiastic singing with those in attendance requesting songs that affirmed the life-changing power of the gospel. Among those would be any number of translators who had come into the city to get supplies before returning to their assigned location in remote tribal villages.

"Uncle Cam" would call on these missionaries to stand and give a report on their work. With joyful expressions and testimony of the tangible evidence of the Spirit's work, these translators would give praise to God and encouragement to the support personnel. Something is refreshingly authentic about eyewitness accounts of God at work.

What was true in a missionary setting half a century ago is no less true today. When we allow for God's people to stand up in the midst of the congregation and tell what they have seen and heard, the church is strengthened and faith grows. Next time you are given an opportunity to bear witness to God's faithfulness in your life, stand and deliver.

I will give thee thanks in the great congregation: I will praise thee among much people.

PSALM 35:18 (KJV)

PRAYER

Think back to times when you heard the "saints" in your home church extol the goodness of the Lord. Allow those memories to grease the skids of your faith as you approach your Father in prayer.

I WILL BLESS THEE, O LORD

With my hands lifted up
And my mouth filled with praise,
With a heart of thanksgiving,
I will bless Thee, O Lord.

I will bless Thee, O Lord;
I will bless Thee, O Lord.
With a heart of thanksgiving,
I will bless Thee, O Lord.

—ESTHER WATANABE

any reasons could be given for why we raise our hands when we praise the Lord. For one thing, it's biblical. The psalm writer invited God's people to lift holy hands in the sanctuary. It's also a physical demonstration of need. We are calling on the Lord and requesting His attention. Besides that, it's a symbol of humility. If, when our hands our extended, our palms are open and facing up, we approach the Lord expressing our emptiness. We are, in a manner of speaking, acknowledging our dependency on Him.

Maybe it helps to think of it like this: When we were in school, the teacher would often ask those who knew the answer to raise their hands. Well, how about it? We who follow Jesus claim that He is the answer to our alienation with God and each other. If we have accepted Jesus' free gift of salvation, we not only *know* the answer, we *have* the answer. It makes sense then, in the context of worship, that we raise our hands high to remind ourselves that we know that the One we worship is the answer to every need we bring with us to church.

If you have been reluctant to raise your hands, why not let yourself go? Be bold. If you know the answer, don't be shy.

Thus will I bless thee while I live: I will lift up my hands in thy name.

PSALM 63:4 (KJV)

PRAYER

Let body language join with the words of your mouth in prayer today. Kneel in the Lord's presence as an indicator of reverence. Lift your hands as a symbol of praise.

ROCK OF MY SALVATION

You are the Rock of my salvation;
You are the strength of my life;
You are my hope and my inspiration;
Lord, unto You will I cry.

I believe in You, believe in You,
For Your faithful love to me.
You have been my help in time of need;
Lord, unto You will I cleave.

—TERESA MULLER

ocks are solid, sure, unmovable. Whether they are part of a strong formation like the Rockies, the awesome depth of the Grand Canyon, or the rugged beauty of the Badlands, we somehow know that they are here to stay. David celebrated that reality by picturing his God as a Rock—offering a certain salvation, strength, hope, and, yes, even inspiration. David spent many years running from a wicked king and hiding in the rock formations of Israel that provided fortresslike protection. Those rocks would prove to be his salvation. For those who feared wild beasts or beastlike robbers, a well-placed chunk of limestone could be a lifesaver.

As we face life's difficult circumstances, God is our Rock. In Him we hide. We trust in Him, knowing that He is immoveable, unshakable, standing forever. As the mountains provided safety for David, so God helps us in our time of need, providing a safe place. Nothing can hurt us when we are standing on our Rock of sure salvation.

The LORD lives! Blessed be my Rock! Let God be exalted, the Rock of my salvation!

2 SAMUEL 22:47 (NKJV)

PRAYER

Since God promises to be our Rock and give us a wall of protection, read a favorite promise you've underlined in your Bible before pouring out your heart to the Lord.

ALL WE LIKE SHEEP

All we, like sheep, have gone astray,
Each of us turning our own separate way.
We have all sinned and fallen short of Your glory,
But Your glory is what we desire to see,
And in Your presence is where we long to be.

O Lord, show us Your mercy and grace;
Take us to Your holy place.
Forgive our sin and heal our land;
We long to live in Your presence once again.

—DON MOEN

yopia. Even though it sounds like utopia, it's a not even close. Myopia is the ultimate condition of nearsightedness. It's a case of looking out for ourselves. And based on what we read in the Bible, it's congenital.

We are all born with this "I" disorder. From the very beginning, we seek our own way, see what we want to see, and close our eyes to others. In all reality, at the center of sin is a preoccupation with "me." That's why sin is sometimes written this way: s-I-n.

But God's vision for our lives is not restricted by our blindness. When we admit our selfish orientation and seek healing, God focuses His grace in our direction with laserlike precision and deals with the "I" of s-I-n. And the beauty of God's remedy is this: It does more than heal our individual situation; it has national implications. When we come before Him as a nation and admit our myopia, He restores our ability to look to Him as the moral compass of our country.

This mellow song draws us into an attitude of contrition and confession. Allow it to move you to identify an "I" infection that may be preventing you from seeing God in all His fullness.

All we like sheep have gone astray; we have turned every one to his own way; and the LORD hath laid on him the iniquity of us all.

ISAIAH 53:6 (KJV)

PRAYER

Pray for your nation. Ask God to show His mercy in grace, not only in your life, but in your land.

MEEKNESS AND MAJESTY (THIS IS YOUR GOD)

Meekness and majesty, manhood and Deity
In perfect harmony, the Man who is God,
Lord of eternity dwells in humanity,
Kneels in humility and washes our feet.

O what a mystery, meekness and majesty!
Bow down and worship, for this is your God;
This is your God.

—GRAHAM KENDRICK

xymorons are word couplets that negate one another. They are paired opposites like "jumbo shrimp," "now then," "genuine copy," and "recorded live." Some of them can be humorous, such as "Microsoft Works," "military intelligence," or "airplane food."

When it comes to describing Jesus, oxymorons are neither funny nor out of the ordinary. We can't seem to come to terms with His identity without allowing for descriptions that defy normal categories. He is the God-Man, the Morning Star, the Suffering Messiah, and the Servant King.

In this wonderful hymn by Graham Kendrick about the Incarnation, we are posed with another oxymoron: Meekness and Majesty. In fact, the lyrics of this song are filled with contrasts. And when you stop and think about it, ours is an oxymoronic faith. The "simple mystery" of salvation is a portrait of opposites. We die in order to live. We give in order to receive. The first shall be last. In poverty we become rich.

Before doing anything else today, why not watch and pray?

For even the Son of Man did not come to be served, but to serve, and to give his life as a ransom for many.

MARK 10:45

PRAYER

Celebrate the mystery of your faith. As difficult as it might be for you, talk to the Lord without needing to understand how prayer works or why He allows what He does.

TO HIM WHO SITS ON THE THRONE

To Him who sits on the throne
And unto the Lamb;
To Him who sits on the throne
And unto the Lamb
Be blessing and glory
And glory and power
Forever.

—DEBBYE GRAAFSMA

t was her dad's fiftieth birthday party. Even though she wanted to stay up, Lauren's mom insisted she go to bed before the company arrived. With the doorbell and all the voices, laughter, and music, the four-year-old could not fall asleep. So when her curiosity could stand it no longer, Lauren slipped out of bed and quietly descended the staircase. To her disappointment, the French doors leading into the living room were closed. Lauren was wise enough to know that it would not be smart to open the doors and walk in. So, stepping up on her tiptoes, the curious child peeked through the keyhole near the door latch. What she saw was unlike any birthday party she'd been to. It was magical!

When it comes to heaven, the writers of the New Testament don't go into specific detail, but they do provide us a keyhole through which we can peek. Far more wonderful than the most elaborate birthday party, heaven promises to be a worship festival that defies words. The music will be breathtaking. The beauty will be thrilling. The glory of God's presence will leave us straining for words. As the old gospel hymn puts it, "What a day of rejoicing that will be!"

In a loud voice they sang: "Worthy is the Lamb, who was slain, to receive power and wealth and wisdom and strength and honor and glory and praise!"

REVELATION 5:12

PRAYER

Think about heaven. Ask God to fill your heart with a desire to go there. Who waits for you there? Thank the Lord for their influence in your life.

H O N O R A N D G L O R Y

To the King eternal, immortal,
Invisible, the only God,
Be the honor and glory
Forever and ever.

Honor and glory forever,
Honor and glory forever,
Honor and glory forever,
Amen.

—GARY OLIVER

ome years ago, a magazine published an issue with breathtaking pictures that were processed in 3-D format. Each copy of that particular issue included a disposable pair of glasses that enabled the viewer to see what was not clear to the naked eye. Those who wore the special lenses were treated to the scenery in impressive detail.

In personal worship we are privileged to draw near to the unseen Christ. When filtered through glorious music and devotional insights, the eyes of faith are able to lock in on evidences of the Lord that might otherwise be missed. Songs like "Honor and Glory" remind us that the God we worship and adore is beyond our ability to see. Nonetheless, He is not beyond experiencing.

The lyrics of this song repeat over and over again. It's not because the writer ran out of words. Rather, it is because repetition helps us focus on the beauty of the Lord's presence in our lives. Repetition helps us meditate and in meditation, our vantage point is improved.

Adore your wonderful Lord, again and again!

Now to the King eternal, immortal, invisible, the only God, be honor and glory for ever and ever. Amen.

1 TIMOTHY 1:17

PRAYER

Take a phrase from this song and repeat it over and over again in your head. Allow the truth of those few words to usher you into the presence of invisible God who desires to reveal Himself to you.

I ' V E   F O U N D   J E S U S

Well I hear they're singing in the streets,
"Jesus is alive!"
And all creation shouts aloud,
"Jesus is alive!"
Now surely we can be all changed 'cause
Jesus is alive,
And everybody here can know that
Jesus is alive.

And I will live for all my days
To raise a banner of truth and light,
To sing about my Savior's love.
And the best thing that happened—
It was the day I met You.
I've found Jesus!

—MARTIN SMITH

uring the Jesus People movement of the seventies, churches of every imaginable denomination joined together in a unified effort to evangelize our country. In a campaign sponsored by Campus Crusade for Christ, believers all over the nation placed bumper stickers on their cars which read, "I Found It!" When curious commuters saw the slogan, it was hoped that they would ask the driver, "What did you find?"

As is often the case, well-intentioned ideas breed cynical or antagonistic responses. Before long, some cars bore bumper stickers that read, "I Never Lost It!" Sadly, those who mocked the joy of finding life's ultimate destination continued down a one-way street in the wrong direction.

After several months the "I Found It!" campaign had run its course, but not before the population of Christ's Kingdom had increased by several thousand. But all these many years later, Jesus continues to be found by those willing to admit that they have a need of Him.

You will seek me and find me when you seek me with all your heart.

JEREMIAH 29:13

PRAYER

Think about the day you met Jesus. Remember how you felt? Thank Him for all He has done for you. Pray for family and friends who still need to meet Him.

T R A D I N G   M Y   S O R R O W S
(Y E S ,   L O R D)

I'm trading my sorrows,

I'm trading my shame,

I'm laying them down

For the joy of the Lord.

I'm trading my sickness,

I'm trading my pain,

I'm laying them down

For the joy of the Lord.

Yes, Lord; yes, Lord; yes, yes, Lord,

Amen.

—DARRELL EVANS

his storm the residents of Naperville, Illinois, continue to talk about. On July 16, 1996, the summer skies opened and refused to close until seventeen inches of rain had fallen. It was a record amount of rainfall. Sump pumps were unable to keep up with the accumulating water in basements. Hundreds of thousands of dollars of furniture and clothing was destroyed. Inflatable rafts allowed neighbors to navigate streets that were too deep with water for cars to drive through.

As is often the case, after the torrential rain, lightning, and thunder had done their damage, the storm moved to the east. The memorable night of unimaginable destruction gave way to a morning of brilliant sunshine and clear blue skies.

According to the psalmist, life is filled with other kinds of storms. The floodgates of pain, sorrow, and fear let loose and drench us with despair. But he quickly adds that the rising of the sun will bring a change in the forecast. Sorrow may last for the night, but joy returns in the morning. If you are in the midst of the flood, grab hold of God and hang on. The end is in sight. Joy will come.

Weeping may endure for a night, but joy comes in the morning.

PSALM 30:5b (NKJV)

PRAYER

Go ahead and admit your pain and fear to the Father. He desires to carry you through the current storm. Trust Him that the weather will soon be changing.

W H Y   S O   D O W N C A S T ?

Why so downcast, O my soul?
Put your hope in God,
put your hope in God,
Put your hope in God.
O why so downcast, O my soul?
Put your hope in God
And bless the Lord, O my soul.

Bless the Lord—
He's the lifter of my countenance.
Bless the Lord—
He's the lifter of my head.
Bless the Lord—
He's the lifter of my countenance.
I will never be ashamed.

—Frank Berrios, Tom Brooks, and Jeff Hamlin

helsea Thomas was born with Moebius Syndrome. No matter how much she wanted to smile, for the first seven years of her life, she couldn't. It was physiologically impossible. Little Chelsea was born without a key nerve that transmits the "smile signal" from her brain to her face. As a result, even when she was happy, her face was sad.

Fortunately for Chelsea, a team of doctors in California operated on the seven-year-old in 1995. They removed a muscle and a nerve from her leg and transplanted them beneath the surface of her face. And as you might imagine, Chelsea Thomas has something to smile about.

Whereas Moebius Syndrome is a very rare condition, unhappy Christians are only too common. We are easily swayed by the circumstances that come our way or our emotional response to those circumstances. The lilting melody and simple lyrics of this song drive home a simple truth: Those who belong to the Lord have no cause to be downcast. Because the Lord has taken responsibility for our lives and our future, we have reason to lift our heads up and be grateful.

Why are you downcast, O my soul? Why so disturbed within me? Put your hope in God, for I will yet praise him, my Savior and my God.

PSALM 42:5, 6

PRAYER

Don't focus on what you need; give praise to the Lord for all He has given you already. Celebrate His faithfulness. And as you pray today, smile.

O N L Y   Y O U

No one but You, Lord,
Can satisfy the longing in my heart.
Nothing I do, Lord,
Can take the place of drawing near to You.

Only You can fill my deepest longing;
Only You can breathe in me new life;
Only You can fill my heart with laughter;
Only You can answer my heart's cry.

Father, I love You;
Come satisfy the longing in my heart.
Fill me, overwhelm me,
Until I know Your love deep in my heart.

—ANDY PARK

few hundred years after Jesus personally taught His disciples about the innate hunger of the human heart for the Father, Augustine personally attested to the same. He wrote, "Thou hast made us for thyself O God, and our hearts are restless until they rest in thee." Many centuries later Blaise Pascal sang his own version of the same song. According to this brilliant philosopher, every person is born with a God-shaped vacuum that He alone can fill.

Everyone who has ever lived has attempted to prove that he or she is the exception to the rule. We seek to fill the hole in our soul with pleasure and power and entertainment and friendship and status and wealth. But in our attempt to be in a league of our own, we find that we have struck out.

Only God can satisfy the longings of our hearts. That's the way He made us. And the reason He did is so that He can have the exclusive joy in making us complete. What's incredibly wonderful is the joy that is ours when we simply quit trying to find our joy outside of Him.

Even strong young lions sometimes go hungry, but those who trust in the LORD will never lack any good thing.

PSALM 34:10 (NLT)

PRAYER

Sit back. Put your feet up. Take deep breaths. Take a few months to accept the fact that you have just cause to rest in the Lord. He is the destination of your life's search.

THE HEART OF WORSHIP

When the music fades, all is stripped away,
And I simply come,
Longing just to bring something that's of worth
That will bless Your heart.

I'll bring You more than a song,
For a song in itself is not what You have required.
You search much deeper within
Through the way things appear;
You're looking into my heart.

I'm coming back to the heart of worship,
And it's all about You, all about You, Jesus.
I'm sorry, Lord, for the thing I've made it,
When it's all about You; it's all about You, Jesus.

—MATT REDMAN

cotty couldn't believe it. His birthday party was a total failure.

He had invited about a dozen boys in his kindergarten class. On Scotty's birthday, each boy came dressed up in his Sunday best bearing a brightly wrapped present. But upon coming through the front door, the invited guests gathered the birthday boy and sang happy birthday while holding on to their gifts. When the song was over, as quickly as they had come, the boys were gone. And they didn't even leave the presents.

As unthinkable as that scenario is, sometimes that's how we approach the Lord's Day. We show up at His house looking a little nicer than we ordinarily do. We come prepared to give Him our hearts. At first everything seems to be on track. We follow the lead of the praise team and sing a medley of worship choruses with feeling and expression. But when the singing stops, it's as if we've disconnected.

It's good to remind ourselves that even though we sometimes refer to "praise singing" as worship, what we do the entire time we are at church is worship. The essence of worship is relating to the one whose day it is. It's all about Him, not just the songs.

Serve the LORD with gladness; come before him with joyful songs.

PSALM 100:2

PRAYER

Ask God to give you a desire to enter into the whole of the worship service this coming Lord's Day. Express your willingness to worship Him in truth as well as in spirited singing.

THE HEART OF WORSHIP

When the music fades, all is stripped away,
And I simply come,
Longing just to bring something that's of worth
That will bless Your heart.

I'll bring You more than a song,
For a song in itself is not what You have required.
You search much deeper within
Through the way things appear;
You're looking into my heart.

I'm coming back to the heart of worship,
And it's all about You, all about You, Jesus.
I'm sorry, Lord, for the thing I've made it,
When it's all about You; it's all about You, Jesus.

—MATT REDMAN

t's all about You, Jesus. We would do well to make that our refrain—not just on Sunday morning during worship, but every day. In essence, for the believer, every day should be "worship-full," for every moment is given to us by God's grace. And if every moment is considered as an opportunity to worship God, then every moment is all about Him.

What an effect it would have on our lives if we stopped and realized, "It's not about me." What peace we will gain when we understand that whatever happens in our lives is because "it's not about me; it's about Him." When things don't go the way we want, we understand that it's not about us, it's about God's bigger picture, God's glory. When we face suffering and difficulty, we understand that it's not about us, it's about Him. Whatever fills our days, whatever God calls us to do in any moment, we can remember that if we do that job, we are doing it for Him because it's all about Him. That infuses whatever we do—even the mundane and ordinary—with eternal significance.

It's not about us; it's about Him.

So whether you eat or drink or whatever you do, do it all for the glory of God.

1 CORINTHIANS 10:31

PRAYER

As you go through your day, consciously remind yourself that your life is not all about you. Instead, it's all about God—serving Him, glorifying Him, sharing Him with your world.

TAKE MY LIFE

Holiness, holiness is what I long for;
Holiness is what I need;
Holiness, holiness is what you want from me.

Faithfulness, faithfulness is what I long for;
Faithfulness is what I need;
Faithfulness, faithfulness is what you want from me.

So take my heart and form it; take my mind, transform it;
Take my will and conform it to yours, to yours, O Lord.

Righteousness, righteousness is what I long for;
Righteousness is what I need;
Righteousness, righteousness is what you want from me.

—SCOTT UNDERWOOD

t's the kind of unrehearsed comment you'd expect to hear on Bill Cosby's *Kids Say the Darnedest Things.* The interviewer was asking children about their career aspirations. When a certain little girl was asked what she wanted to do "when she got big like her mommy," she replied, "Go on a diet!"

Sometimes the thoughts we have about our future goals are different than what God has in mind. He isn't all that concerned about our career or geographic plans or our retirement dreams. His desires for our tomorrows have more to do with the kinds of people we are becoming inside. The color of the collar we wear to work isn't nearly as important to Him as the content of our character.

As we stand with our backs to His spiritual growth chart, He measures the degree to which our hearts need to be formed, our minds need to be transformed, and our wills need to be conformed. It's a measuring process that occurs every day for the rest of our lives.

The key, of course, is to let God do His work, to say to Him daily, "Take my life . . . all of it!"

Do not conform any longer to the pattern of this world, but be transformed by the renewing of your mind.

ROMANS 12:2

PRAYER

Review the qualities of the fruit of the Spirit (Galatians 5:22, 23). Ask God to evaluate each quality while you quietly listen in His presence for His response.

A R M S   O F   L O V E

I sing a simple song of love
To my Savior, to my Jesus.
I'm grateful for the things You've done,
My loving Savior, O precious Jesus.
My heart is glad
That You've called me Your own,
'Cause there's no place I'd rather be
Than in Your arms of love,
In Your arms of love,
Holding me still, holding me near
In Your arms of love.

—CRAIG MUSSEAU

here's no place I'd rather be than in your arms of love." We love the way those sweet lyrics sound. But the truth is, there are times when we aren't aware that that's exactly where we are.

You most likely have read "Footprints in the Sand." That inspiring poem was written by Margaret Powers. In it, she describes the plight of a person who felt abandoned by God in his or her darkest hour only to discover that he or she wasn't abandoned at all. The single set of footprints didn't belong to the person in pain walking the beach alone. They were the Lord's. The reason there was only one set was because the person in crisis was being carried.

Margaret Powers has lived the truth of her verse. Shortly after writing "Footprints," her poem was stolen and distributed throughout the world. For over two decades, the poet received neither recognition nor royalties. At long last, her ownership of the poem was proven. Looking back on this grave injustice, Margaret attests to the "arms of love" that held her. Although some days she didn't feel the Lord close, He never let her down. Perhaps you can relate.

Even to your old age and gray hairs I am he, I am he who will sustain you. I have made you and I will carry you; I will sustain you and I will rescue you.

ISAIAH 46:4

PRAYER

Rest in the arms of the Lord. Thank Him for those everlasting arms that never tire or lose their strength.

B R E A T H E

This is the air I breathe,
This is the air I breathe,
Your Holy presence living in me.
This is my daily bread,
This is my daily bread,
Your very Word spoken to me.

And I,
I'm desperate for you.
And I,
I'm lost without you.

—MARIE BARNETT

he air is charged with emotion. Bystanders feel the negative energy. Desperate young parents are frantically searching a large downtown department store for their two-year-old child. Somehow, somewhere, their baby wandered off when they were looking at new furniture. Store security is collecting information from the panicked parents, all the while attempting to calm them. Strangers join the search efforts.

Without warning, a grandmotherly woman walks into view with the child in her arms. The sudden heroine has saved the day. But even as the little boy's eyes meet his mother's, he continues to sob uncontrollably. The fear he has felt thinking that he has lost his mommy and daddy is all consuming. Between heaves and sobs, he literally struggles to take in a breath.

No doubt you've seen a similar scene. Your heart goes out to both the child and the parents. But have you ever pictured yourself as a lost child desperately fighting to breathe, all the while longing for the arms of your heavenly Father? That is a poignant portrait of our dependence on God that we never outgrow.

Run to His arms . . . and take a breath!

As the deer pants for streams of water, so my soul pants for you, O God. My soul thirsts for God, for the living God. When can I go and meet with God?

PSALM 42:1, 2

PRAYER

Draw near to the Lord as to a parent. Cast yourself on Him as one who cares for you and longs to hold you. Share with Him your deepest need.

D A Y 8 8

E T E R N I T Y

I will be yours, you will be mine
Together in eternity.
Our hearts of love will be entwined
Together in eternity,
Forever in eternity.

No more tears of pain
In our eyes,
No more fear or shame,
For we will be with You;
Yes, we will be with You.

—BRIAN DOERKSON

he story is told about a man and his teenage son who lived in a little village in Spain. One night the man and the teenager had a disagreement that left them both feeling betrayed. The next morning when the father went to Paco's room to awaken him, he noticed that the boy's bed had not been slept in. The boy had run away.

A lump rose to the father's throat and refused to be swallowed. His son meant more to him than anything. The thought of being separated from his boy was too much for the man. Wanting to make amends and begin again, the father went to the post office in town and tacked up a large sign that read, "Paco, all is forgiven. I love you. Meet me here tomorrow. Papa."

The next day the father went to the post office hoping to be reunited with his son. To his amazement, in addition to his Paco, six other teenage boys by the same name stood there, each answering a call for love, each hoping it was his dad inviting him home.

Jesus' story of the prodigal son is more than just a parable. It is a story lived out in every generation in every culture. In fact, it is every person's story. It is an amazing story of a God who waits for our return to His open arms.

If you ever leave "home," remember your loving Father who waits and longs for your return.

"Let's have a feast and celebrate. For this son of mine was dead and is alive again; he was lost and is found." So they began to celebrate.
LUKE 15:23b, 24

PRAYER

Rewind your memory tape to your own rebellion from the Father and then replay the scene of falling into His arms. Thank God for His grace, mercy, and the promise of eternity with Him.

177

W E   R E M E M B E R   Y O U

As we drink this cup,

We worship You.

As we eat this bread,

We honor You.

And we offer You our lives

As You have offered Yours for us.

We remember

All You've done for us.

We remember

Your covenant with us.

We remember

And worship You, O Lord.

—Rick Founds

memory-challenged fifty-year-old once wrote in his journal: "I've reached the age where once again I play at hide-and-seek. My playmates aren't the kids next door but facts I try to speak. It irks me so to know I know a certain name or face, but when I think I'm getting warm they're gone without a trace. So much of what I once recalled gets stuck inside my mind. Like popcorn hulls between my teeth, some thoughts get caught, I find. But gratefully, it's just a game. It's not a total loss. I'd do just fine if I could find a string of mental floss."

Forgetfulness doesn't just come with age. It's a consequence of living in a fallen world. We are born with a tendency to forget what God has done for us. That's why He made sure His people had visual aids and tangible memory joggers in both the Old and New Testaments. The ultimate symbolic memory aid is Communion, the Lord's Supper. It calls to mind the priceless investment God made to provide us the free gift of eternal salvation.

As you come to the table, remember what your Father did in sending Jesus and remember what Jesus did on the Cross.

And when he had given thanks, he broke it and said, "This is my body, which is for you; do this in remembrance of me."

1 CORINTHIANS 11:24

PRAYER

As you pray, look around the room at objects and mementoes that call to mind God's blessings in your life. Take several moments to remember His goodness.

L A M B   O F   G O D

Your only Son no sin to hide,
But You have sent Him from Your side
To walk upon this guilty sod
And to become the Lamb of God.

Your gift of love they crucified;
They laughed and scorned Him as He died.
The humble King they named a fraud
And sacrificed the Lamb of God.

O Lamb of God, sweet Lamb of God,
I love the holy Lamb of God.
O wash me in His precious blood—
My Jesus Christ, the Lamb of God.

I was so lost I should have died,
But You have brought me to Your side
To be led by Your staff and rod
And to be called a lamb of God.

—TWILA PARIS

n technologically savvy America, the landscape of most people's lives is not dotted with wooly sheep and bleating lambs. The pastoral scenes that once defined us are hung in galleries of history. About the only reference to sheep that remains a part of our vocabulary is that of "counting" them when we can't fall asleep.

Picturing Jesus as the Lamb of God is a bit of a shock to sophisticated minds. Yet it is this other-than-expected image that jars us from a culture of comfort and convenience and forces us to return to the world of the Bible.

Only as we enter into the mindset of the ancient Hebrews can we fully understand how Jesus is the Lamb of God. The smell of wet wool and dried blood was part of their life. The unmistakable aroma of roasted lamb and burnt flesh was essential to their faith. Innocent and helpless lambs were butchered as part of God's remedy for sin—until He offered His Son as the once-and-for-all sacrifice. Because of Him, the most innocent of all who have ever lived, children's pets could now be spared. But far more importantly, God's children could now live forever.

Jesus, the Lamb of God, *your* Lamb, died so that you could live.

The next day John saw Jesus coming toward him and said, "Look, the Lamb of God, who takes away the sin of the world!"

JOHN 1:29

PRAYER

Thank Jesus, the precious Lamb of God who took away the world's sin. Thank Him for letting you, a little sheep, join His flock and be led by Him.

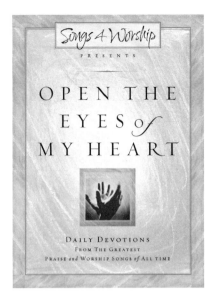

A beautiful, full-color daily devotional that will lead you into the presence of God, Open the Eyes of My Heart *features 90 more spiritually moving devotionals based on the greatest praise and worship songs of all time.*
ISBN 1-59145-021-7

An inspiring companion volume, The Sacrifice of Praise *tells the fascinating stories behind the creation of the greatest praise and worship songs of all time.*
ISBN 1-59145-014-4

Available wherever books are sold.